Marbury v. Madison

LANDMARK LAW CASES
&
AMERICAN SOCIETY

Peter Charles Hoffer
N. E. H. Hull
Williamjames Hull Hoffer
Series Editors

For a complete list of titles in the series go to www.kansaspress.ku.edu

WILLIAM E. NELSON

Marbury v.
Madison

The Origins and Legacy

of Judicial Review

Second Edition, Revised and Expanded

UNIVERSITY PRESS OF KANSAS

© 2018 by the University Press of Kansas
All rights reserved

Published by the University Press of Kansas (Lawrence, Kansas 66045), which was
organized by the Kansas Board of Regents and is operated and funded by Emporia
State University, Fort Hays State University, Kansas State University, Pittsburg State
University, the University of Kansas, and Wichita State University

Library of Congress Cataloging-in-Publication Data

Names: Nelson, William E. (William Edward), 1940– author.
Title: Marbury v. Madison : the origins and legacy of judicial review / William E.
Nelson.
Description: Second edition, revised and expanded. | Lawrence : University Press
of Kansas, 2018. | Series: Landmark law cases & American society | Includes
bibliographical references and index. Identifiers: LCCN 2018004640
ISBN 9780700626533 (hardback)
ISBN 9780700626403 (paperback)
ISBN 9780700626410 (ebook)
Subjects: LCSH: Judicial review—United States—History. | Separation of powers—
United States—History. | Marbury, William, 1761 or 1762–1835—Trials, litigation,
etc. | Madison, James, 1751–1836—Trials, litigation, etc. | BISAC:
LAW / Constitutional. | HISTORY / United States / 19th Century. | HISTORY /
United States / Colonial Period (1600–1775).
Classification: LCC KF4575 .N45 2018 | DDC 347.73/12—dc23.
LC record available at https://lccn.loc.gov/2018004640.

British Library Cataloguing-in-Publication Data is available.

Printed in the United States of America
10 9 8 7 6 5 4 3 2 1

The paper used in this publication is recycled and contains 30 percent postconsumer
waste. It is acid free and meets the minimum requirements of the American National
Standard for Permanence of Paper for Printed Library Materials z39.48-1992.

To Elaine, Leila, Gregory,

and the Rule of Law

CONTENTS

At first glance, one might wonder why such an old chestnut as *Marbury v. Madison* would merit inclusion in a modern series on landmark cases. After all, not only is the doctrine that the highest court in the land has the duty as well as the authority to decide on the constitutionality of federal and state legislation almost two hundred years old, it has been confirmed innumerable times. The case itself was decided by a unanimous court and did not bring about a revolution in the legal system or the politics of the times. Indeed, its author, Chief Justice John Marshall, crafted it to avoid a direct encounter between the Federalists on the US Supreme Court and President Thomas Jefferson and his new Republican majority in Congress.

The fact remains that the case is an essential part of the adolescence of American democratic republicanism, for in it the Court upheld the rule of law without calling into question the electoral revolution that turned the Federalists out of office and brought in the Jeffersonian Republicans. Marshall and his court also protected the independence of the judiciary and the High Court at a time when these institutions were under attack. Thus, the legacy of the case is not only its doctrinal contribution of judicial review to American constitutionalism but its proof that the Court could remain, if not above all political considerations, at least safe from overt partisanship.

This was no easy task, for as Professor Nelson so incisively demonstrates, Marshall faced two dangers. The first was the Republican animus for a Federalist-dominated judiciary. The second was the temptation to use the courts to further the Federalist program. This included a strong central government and strong courts. Marshall succumbed to neither the fear of the first nor the allure of the second. By insisting upon the traditional view that the task of courts was one of discovering rather than making law, he placed the decision of the Supreme Court out of the reach of both parties.

But later American courts, in a different political context, have changed the way in which judicial review functions. In an age when the consensus that eighteenth-century Anglo-American elites shared has given way to the politics of interest groups, Nelson argues, we have come to see courts as policy-making bodies weighing the competing interests behind the cases brought to the bar. Thus, for us, judicial review becomes something that would be quite foreign to Marshall—a final balancing of the interests.

This is an exciting book, broad in scope and daring in conception. It combines legal history, constitutional theory, and political science. In the final chapter, Nelson goes beyond the boundaries of the United States to apply the lessons of *Marbury* to nations that did not exist when Marshall handed down his decision. For now, these new states face the same issues of law and politics, constitutionalism and partisanship, that Marshall understood so well.

ACKNOWLEDGMENTS

My work on this book, as well as the articles and the chapter of another book from which parts of this book are derived, has resulted in the accumulation of many debts. The research staff of the New York University Law Library fulfilled every request for materials that I presented to it, and the Nassau County Public Library System, which has an excellent American history collection, was equally helpful. I am especially indebted to Ronald Brown, Elizabeth Evans, and Gretchen Feltes, reference librarians at the NYU Law Library, and to Jeffrey Mason, a former reference librarian at the Hewlett-Woodmere Public Library.

I wish to acknowledge permission from Oxford University Press to reprint portions of chapter 7 of William E. Nelson, *The Common Law in Colonial America*, vol. 4: *Law and the Constitution on the Eve of Independence, 1735–1776* (New York: Oxford University Press, 2018). I also acknowledge permission to reprint portions of the following articles:

William E. Nelson, "The Eighteenth-Century Background of John Marshall's Constitutional Jurisprudence," *Michigan Law Review* 76 (1978): 893.

William E. Nelson, "History and Neutrality in Constitutional Adjudication," *Virginia Law Review* 72 (1986): 1237.

William E. Nelson, "Changing Conceptions of Judicial Review: The Evolution of Constitutional Theory in the States, 1790–1860," *University of Pennsylvania Law Review* 120 (1972): 1166.

Footnotes are available in the earlier chapter and articles.

A draft of the first edition of this book was presented to the Legal History Colloquium at New York University School of Law, and I am indebted to all of its participants for their helpful comments and criticisms, but especially to R. B. Bernstein, Mark Brilliant, Barry Friedman, William LaPiana, and Howard Venable. Thomas Mackey read a draft of the second edition and offered helpful suggestions. My former colleagues Bruce Ackerman, Christopher Eisgruber, and Larry Kramer each contributed in significant ways to the refinement of my thinking as I wrote early articles on *Marbury* and judicial review and then transformed the earlier articles into a book. The late

Edward Weinfeld, himself a judge of the same Olympian qualities as John Marshall, had for years urged me to turn my article on Marshall's constitutional jurisprudence into a book, and he thereby made me especially receptive when Peter Hoffer offered me the opportunity to do so. Hoffer's patient editing and suggestions improved both editions of the book, as did the reader's reports of G. Edward White on both editions and David Thomas Konig and Charles F. Hobson on the second edition. David Congdon, an acquisitions editor at the University Press of Kansas, was especially helpful in positioning this volume in the Landmark Law Cases series.

I also owe an immeasurable debt of gratitude to John Sexton, who made New York University School of Law the best place in the world for the scholarly study of law in general and of legal history in particular. Generous support for the writing of both the first and second editions of this book was provided by the Filomen D'Agostino and Max E. Greenberg Faculty Research Fund of New York University School of Law. I thank Lisa Koederitz and Shirley Gray for all their assistance in shepherding both editions of the book, and Dennis Garcia for his research assistance on the second edition.

I have dedicated the book to my family—my wife, Elaine; my daughter, Leila; and my son, Gregory—because of the relationship between their lives and the principal subject of this book: the origins of the rule of law. With help from Muslim friends and a female Muslim judge who urged us to get Leila out of the country quickly, Elaine and I spent seven weeks in 1974 adopting Leila in Iran, when it was ruled by a shah and secret police rather than law. We learned of young people who had protested against the regime being taken from their parents' homes and never seen again. When Leila's adoption was completed, we congratulated ourselves on saving her from an authoritarian police state and bringing her to safety in rule-of-law America. Four years later we adopted Gregory, who has a Native American genetic heritage, from Guatemala, again with confidence that the rule of law would guarantee his safety in America.

The rule of law is now under challenge, however, and our confidence in our children's safety is shaken. As any reader of the pages that follow will see, I, for one, recognize the limitations of courts and law—in particular, the incapacity of constitutional law to provide full social justice to discrete and insular minorities. The power of the political process is required to achieve true equality and justice for all. But the rule of law nonetheless serves the important end for which Elaine and I brought Leila and Gregory to America—security and the protection of liberty. The rule of law is a true conservative value. But will Americans support it? In the years to come, people of Leila and Gregory's generation, as well as people who are younger, will need to decide whether to urge judges to fight to keep America under the rule of law or to continue pressing judges to create a more perfect world, perhaps at the cost, however, of further undermining the one we have long enjoyed.

Woodmere, New York
September 2017

Introduction

When I first wrote a book about *Marbury v. Madison* nearly two decades ago, I called the case "foundational." Indeed, I thought at the time and continue to think that, along with *Brown v. Board of Education*, *Marbury* is one of the two most significant cases that the Supreme Court of the United States has ever decided. Like everyone else who has written about the case, I concluded that its importance lay in it being the first case in which the Supreme Court "explicitly ruled . . . that it possessed what we now call the power of judicial review, or jurisdiction to examine whether legislation enacted by Congress is consistent with the Constitution."

I have spent most of the last fifteen years studying and writing about the legal and constitutional history of Great Britain's thirteen North American colonies. My research has been published in four volumes under the title *The Common Law in Colonial America*. In this work, I have concluded that the power of courts to review the constitutionality of legislation was well established in the United States by the end of the colonial period. *Marbury v. Madison* achieved nothing new or foundational in declaring that the Supreme Court possessed that power.

Nonetheless, *Marbury* still remains foundational. This book asks why *Marbury* is still so important and offers a new understanding of the significance of the case. That new understanding rests, in turn, upon an appreciation that the Supreme Court's approach to its decision-making process in *Marbury* was almost the polar opposite of its approach to judicial review cases today.

Today we understand that, in deciding whether or not to invalidate an act of a coordinate legislative body, a court inevitably must choose between competing social policies. We believe, for example, that when the Supreme Court decides whether to allow Congress to adopt a law giving different tax treatment to married same-sex couples than it gives to married heterosexual couples, the Court must make an inevitable policy choice about the treatment to be accorded to same-sex marriage. This tenet that constitutional decisions by the Supreme Court necessarily involve policy choice originated in progressive and legal realist critiques of the Court early in the twentieth century. Over time these critiques resulted in what, until recently, has remained the conventional wisdom about *Marbury*, judicial review, and the Marshall Court.

This conventional wisdom, articulated by progressive historians and legal scholars ranging from Albert Beveridge, Robert G. McCloskey, and J. M. Sosin to Felix Frankfurter and Charles Warren, contended that John Marshall, in deciding *Marbury*, consciously furthered the political goals of the Federalist Party, to which he had belonged—first, by stretching the Constitution's meaning to increase national power at the expense of state power, and, second, by designing constitutional doctrines, such as judicial review, that protected the upper classes' privileges against the growing democratic onslaught that in 1829 finally placed Andrew Jackson in the White House.

Frankfurter arguably expressed the conventional view most clearly when he declared in his 1937 book *The Commerce Clause under Marshall, Taney and Waite* that the deepest article of Marshall's faith was the need for a strong central government, not because the Constitution requires it but because such a government would become "the indispensable bulwark of the solid elements of the nation." This conventional wisdom continues even today to claim adherents. In one article, for example, Christopher Eisgruber has advanced an eloquent argument that Marshall's interpretation of the Constitution as a bulwark of national judicial power reflected a policy judgment that the national judiciary was an institution well suited to promoting the happiness and prosperity of the American people.

Nonetheless, during the past several decades, the conventional wisdom has begun to come under attack. Beginning with my own essay "The Eighteenth-Century Background of John Marshall's Constitutional Jurisprudence," historians have advanced new explanations by focusing on what, once it is stated, is obvious—that Marshall and his contemporaries, like all historical actors, understood only the world in which they grew to maturity and could not foresee the future. As James O'Fallon has observed, we need to understand *Marbury* as a case "born of the bitter political battle of its time" and should not credit its author, Chief Justice Marshall, "with foresight that would honor an oracle." If we are to comprehend *Marbury* and the Marshall Court, in short, we need to situate them in the context of eighteenth-century legal and political theory, not in the ideological matrix of twentieth- and twenty-first-century progressivism and legal realism.

It must be stated emphatically that few, if any, Americans in the decades before and after 1800 believed that policy choice should be an inherent element in judicial decision making. Such was not the understanding of the framers who drafted the Constitution at the Philadelphia Convention in 1787 or secured its ratification during the year thereafter. Nor was it the understanding of the Marshall Court when it handed down *Marbury v. Madison*. The framers of the Constitution and the justices who decided *Marbury* understood that only an entity possessing sovereignty—that is, the power to make the ultimate policy choices inherent in changing or creating law—could resolve policy questions. Courts, which did not possess sovereignty, could only find the law as it already existed.

But political thinkers in late eighteenth-century America also had been witness to a decades-long battle over the proper location of sovereignty—a battle that had culminated in war and other momentous political events. Classical British political theory, especially as articulated by William Blackstone in his leading treatise, *Commentaries on the Laws of England*, which was published during the 1760s, posited that sovereignty lay with the king in Parliament: that is, only the House of Commons, the House of Lords, and the Crown, acting together in conjunction, could change the law by enacting legislation. But when Parliament gave vent to this theory in the Declaratory Act of 1766, which stated that the king in Parliament could make laws binding on its American colonies in all cases whatsoever, Americans objected. In their view, Parliament could not be their sovereign, since they lacked representation therein.

For the next nine years, Britain persisted in its claim of parliamentary sovereignty over its colonies, and Americans persisted in their rejection of the claim. Finally, in 1776, Americans declared their independence. Although the Declaration of Independence did not definitively establish the locus of sovereignty, most Americans of the Revolutionary generation assumed that sovereignty lay in the newly independent state legislatures.

Granting full sovereignty to the states, however, left the national government weak, and by the mid-1780s leaders who would come to be known as Federalists began a campaign that culminated in the drafting and ratification of the federal Constitution and in the establishment in 1789 of the federal government. During that campaign, they frequently had to address the issue of sovereignty. They could not leave sovereignty with the states, since state sovereignty made the national government too weak, nor could they place sovereignty in the national government, since Americans who had fought a Revolutionary War against a centralized sovereign government remained too fearful of power to establish a new sovereign national state. During the ratification debates, some Federalists made the intellectual leap of urging that sovereignty lay with the people, not with any governmental body.

There is no need for the purposes of this book to resolve the question of where, in the view of most Americans in the early 1800s, sovereignty—the power to make or change law through the resolution of issues of social policy—lay. If any institution of government was thought in 1803 to possess sovereignty, surely it was not the Supreme Court of the United States. Thus, no one could have thought that the Court, in asserting the power of judicial review, was assuming jurisdiction to make the choices of social policy that only a sovereign could make. In deciding *Marbury v. Madison*, Chief Justice Marshall and his colleagues thus were doing something other than adopting judicial review as we now know it at the beginning of the twenty-first century.

Recent historians and constitutional theorists have offered several suggestions about what the Marshall Court was doing, all of which capture part of reality. One useful book by Charles Hobson, who has been working for many years on a multivolume edition of John Marshall's papers, situates *Marbury* and Marshall's career in the shift from the classical republican political culture of the Revolutionary era, which emphasized the good of the community as a whole, to a liberal political culture emphasizing individual rights and freedom, which was more or less in place by 1840. Most historians probably would reject Hobson's thesis, since the current wisdom in the profession doubts whether eighteenth-century republicanism differed enough from nineteenth-century liberalism to give either concept much explanatory power. Even if one accepts the current wisdom, however, Hobson's book still has special value as a result of the author's access to information about John Marshall, his Court, and his jurisprudence that no other scholar possesses.

Sylvia Snowiss has authored a second book that places Marshall's *Marbury* decision in a late eighteenth-century context. Her argument draws a distinction between ordinary law, which she claims was routinely enforced in the courts, and fundamental law, such as a constitution, which, in her view, could not be enforced by courts but only by electoral or other political action, ultimately by revolution. Snowiss is surely correct in recognizing that important leaders, such as Thomas Jefferson, author of the Declaration of Independence and future president, understood that the people themselves could enforce fundamental law—a view most Americans no longer hold. But, as we shall see in chapter 1, she underestimates the role of popular law-finding, through the institution of the jury, in the enforcement of ordinary law. Moreover, her distinction, although useful in explaining why the doctrine of judicial review enunciated in *Marbury v. Madison* differed radically from the sort of judicial review practiced by courts today, does not identify the element in the eighteenth-century background of *Marbury* that enabled John Marshall to assert, as he did, the power of the Supreme Court to enforce fundamental law. Snowiss's book, in the end, offers a strong, implicit critique of the sort of broad-ranging, policy-oriented judicial review practiced by many constitutional courts today, rather than an explanation of how the practice came into being historically.

A third book, by Robert Lowry Clinton, does offer such an explanation. Clinton interprets *Marbury* in light of Blackstone's principles of statutory construction, the most relevant of which allowed judges to ignore a statute if its application would result in absurdity, repugnancy, or impossibility of performance, but denied the judiciary power to revise or repeal statutes on grounds of policy. Clinton establishes that American ideas about judicial power at the time of *Marbury* were consistent with Blackstone's principles and that those ideas changed, so as to allow judicial invalidation of legislation on constitutional policy grounds, only at the end of the nineteenth century. I do not disagree with Clinton's interpretation, do not question that Blackstonian analytical principles were in the air at the time the Supreme Court decided the *Marbury* case, and do not doubt that those principles may have played some role in Marshall's crafting of his opinion. But they do not account for his decision.

The most important recent book is Larry D. Kramer's *The People Themselves: Popular Constitutionalism and Judicial Review*. Kramer shows persuasively that the general public debated constitutional issues repeatedly during the second half of the eighteenth century—issues ranging from the power of Parliament to tax the colonies and regulate colonial life to the form of state constitutions, the adoption of the federal Constitution, and the power of Congress to charter a national bank and regulate political speech. These issues produced a vast amount of printed literature, including such tracts as the *Federalist Papers*; extralegal meetings such as the Continental Congress and the 1787 Constitutional Convention; riotous activity such as the Boston Tea Party; and ultimately the War for Independence. Kramer sees judicial activity during the course of these events as merely a minor part of a vast popular constitutional movement. His history all points toward a normative conclusion—that today's Supreme Court should return the Constitution to the people by deferring to popular judgments on the Constitution's meaning and not imposing the justices' own interpretations in regard to divisive social issues.

My goals and interests in this book are different. Unlike Kramer and prior scholars such as Sylvia Snowiss and the progressive historians, I am not striving to evaluate whether the Marshall Court usurped power or otherwise made a wrong decision in asserting the power of judicial review in *Marbury*. Like Snowiss, as well as Clinton and Hobson, I do believe that judicial review in *Marbury*, which granted judges authority to decide only issues of law and directed them to avoid political decision making, differed significantly from judicial review as it is practiced today, when judges frequently make choices of policy. But, unlike Hobson, I am not concerned whether Marshall's decision in *Marbury* was consistent with classical, eighteenth-century political thought, and, unlike Clinton, I am not

6

concerned whether the decision was consistent with technical legal doctrines of the Blackstone era.

My main objective is neither to criticize nor to praise *Marbury v. Madison*. Rather, my goal is to assist readers in understanding the decision as a step in the ongoing elaboration of American and, more recently, global constitutionalism. In particular, I hope to establish something different from what other historians have shown—namely, how the Marshall Court, in deciding *Marbury*, was striving to preserve what the justices and nearly all their fellow citizens found best in eighteenth-century constitutionalism, while at the same time accommodating that constitutionalism to new nineteenth-century political realities. I also will attempt in the closing chapters of the book to explain how *Marbury*-style judicial review, which was grounded on a distinction between law and politics, was transformed over the next century and a half into today's judicial review, which we understand inevitably requires judges to resolve contentious issues of constitutional social policy.

My narrative begins with an analysis of the constitutional polity of eighteenth-century colonial British North America. I make two central claims—the first in chapter 1 and the second in chapter 2. The first claim is that coercive power in colonial America was situated mainly in local, usually county, courts and that judges and juries in those courts frequently nullified legislation and other commands of central political authorities. My second claim, however counterintuitive it may seem to Americans at the outset of the twenty-first century, is that mid-eighteenth-century American colonials did not want any government entity to engage in social policy choice. They understood law as fixed and immutable, not as something that government could change in response to shifting conceptions of social good. Indeed, they equated fixed law with liberty, and changeable law with arbitrary rule and tyranny.

From there I move on in chapter 3 to James Otis's initial articulation of the doctrine of judicial review in the *Writs of Assistance Case*. My argument is that Otis was simply describing the practice, with which he was familiar, of judicial and jury nullification of statutes and other central political commands. Having articulated the doctrine in 1761, Otis then disseminated it widely in his 1764 pamphlet, *The Rights of the British Colonies Asserted and Proved*. Chapter 4 next shows how several colonial judges and lawyers used the doctrine in 1765–1766 in holding the Stamp Act unconstitutional. Chapter 5 turns to judicial review cases in the states following the War of Independence, as well as to the implicit adoption of judicial review at the federal level in the 1787 Constitutional Convention.

Chapter 2, as noted above, focuses on colonial understandings about the fixed nature of law and the undesirability of policy choice. However, during the four decades between the end of the Seven Years' War with France in 1763 and the decision of *Marbury v. Madison* in 1803, Americans engaged in debate with advocates of parliamentary sovereignty, declared their independence, fought a war to establish it, drafted and ratified new constitutions, and put new governments into operation. And, for the first time in American history, the election of 1800 peacefully transferred power from a political group advocating one set of social policies to a rival party advocating opposing policies. Thus, by 1803, the American public could not avoid recognition of the fact that law sometimes did change as a result of policy choice.

But public understanding that some legal change was inevitable did not mean that people found change desirable or that they expected significant amounts of change to continue to occur. Americans still understood that liberty was founded upon fixed and immutable law, however much the democratic political process might debate policy choice and produce social change. The core thesis of this book, examined in chapter 8, is that, in *Marbury v. Madison*, Chief Justice John Marshall drew a line, which nearly all citizens of his time believed ought to be drawn, between the legal and the political—between those matters that most Americans agreed were fixed and immutable, and thus subject to legal control, and those matters open to fluctuation and change, and thus the subjects of democratic politics.

Although the Supreme Court lost some power by withdrawing from political decision making, its withdrawal coincidentally strengthened the law. Before *Marbury*, courts were merely one more government entity performing the same legal-political functions that all other entities performed. After *Marbury*, in contrast, courts and law became distinctive and special, superior to and capable of invalidating political decisions in regard to matters subject to the law. In a sense, *Marbury v. Madison* thus accomplished what jurists have long assumed it accomplished—it did not establish judicial review, which was already in place, but over time it created the concept of the rule of law as a mechanism capable of controlling excesses generated in the democratic political process.

Marbury's immediate effect was to protect private property from political interference. The vast majority of adult white men in early nineteenth-century America either already owned land or expected to acquire land at some point during their lives. Moreover, they understood that the law protected and should protect ownership rights. Although they also understood that the law regulated property rights, little demand existed at the time for regulation of a redistributive nature. Thus, when the Marshall Court indicated in dictum in *Marbury v. Madison* that the Constitution and its rule of law barred political actors from interfering with rights akin to the right of property in land, virtually all Americans agreed that the Court's decision was correct.

For more than a century after *Marbury*, judges continued to protect private property, as they had always done. In doing so, they could understand that they were preserving the law of property as something fixed and immutable—that they were upholding Marshall's distinction between law and politics. But as vast accumulations of commercial wealth, which conferred monopoly power on its holders and enabled them to dominate others' lives, grew in the late nineteenth century, demands for redistributive regulation grew, and those who demanded the new regulation came to see the judiciary's constitutional protection of established rights as controversial and political rather than as legal and immutable. For some Americans, at least, Marshall's distinction between law and politics began to dissolve, and judicial review, as shown in chapter 10, began to pass into the realm of policy choice.

The demand for redistributive regulation triumphed during the New Deal, and beginning in 1937, New Dealers remade the Supreme Court. Chapter 11 shows how the Court, in turn, made the political choice to abandon its traditional protection of property rights and to enter upon a new role of safeguarding discrete and insular racial, religious, and cultural minorities who could not protect themselves through majoritarian democratic politics. This new role, in turn, involved the Court in the ad hoc balancing of the policy claims put forth by minorities against the claims of legislative majorities.

Thus, judicial review as we know it today came to fruition. And, as chapter 12 shows, it has spread throughout a world that never shared John Marshall's concern in *Marbury v. Madison* about how to distinguish law from politics, but that, like twenty-first-century America, struggles continuously with the issue of reconciling the rights of ethnic, religious, and cultural minorities with the power of dominant political majorities. A conclusion examines the relationship between the changing function of judicial review and the role of policy choice in the judicial process.

CHAPTER ONE

The Localized Structure of Power

When the thirteen colonies of British North America were first founded in the seventeenth century, their provincial governments had exercised significant power. They had established structures of central governance, created institutions of local government, and legislated substantive law, sometimes in the form of complete codes of law. But, as the colonies grew in population and spread out geographically, provincial governments grew weaker.

By the middle of the eighteenth century, eleven of the thirteen colonies had governors appointed by the Crown or by proprietors in England, and only two, Connecticut and Rhode Island, had elected governors. Because the appointed governors typically had no local political base, they were weak and dependent on another institution of provincial government—the legislature, which possessed some important powers. Its most critical was the power of the purse. Only the legislature could vote to raise taxes needed to pay the governor's and other officials' salaries and to fund any special undertakings, such as wars, in which the governor or Crown officials in London wished to engage. Eighteenth-century legislatures also adopted many private bills, but they rarely enacted general, colony-wide legislation.

As a result, by the eighteenth century, courts had become the main institution of government. Eighteenth-century government, unlike government today, did not consist of a ubiquitous bureaucracy with clear chains of command reaching upward to central political authorities. There were no police, state or local; no department of motor vehicles; no highway department; no state education bureaucracy. There were no colonial equivalents, on any level of government, to the Internal Revenue Service or the Social Security Administration.

Because there was no modern bureaucracy, the judiciary and officials like sheriffs responsible to it were the primary link between a colony's central government and its outlying localities. The judiciary alone could coerce individuals by punishing crimes and imposing money judgments. In some colonies, the judiciary was virtually the whole of local government, but even in colonies where other officials were available, those officials were subject to judicial control. As one member of Congress observed in an end-of-the-century recapitulation, "other departments of the Government" may have been "more splendid," but only the "courts of justice [came] home to every man's habitation."

Courts, in turn, were under local control in every colony, except perhaps Pennsylvania.

In six of the colonies—Connecticut, Maryland, Massachusetts, New Hampshire, New Jersey, and Rhode Island—juries were the vehicle through which localities controlled the judiciary. In these six colonies, juries determined not only the facts of cases but the law applicable to those facts as well.

In American courts of today, judges restrict the evidence juries are permitted to hear and deliver charges or instructions on the law. Judges in Maryland and New Jersey and to a lesser extent in New England used demurrers (pleas by litigants claiming that the pleadings of their opponents were insufficient as a matter of law) and demurrers to the evidence (objections by litigants that evidence offered by their opponents was insufficient to support their legal claims) to try to limit the evidence jurors could hear. And judges in all six colonies had power to deliver instructions from the bench. But these mechanisms often proved to be ineffective tools to control juries. Demurrers and demurrers to the evidence were ineffective because jurors often came to court with knowledge about the cases they would hear. Instructions were ineffective for two reasons.

First, instructions often were contradictory. One potential source of contradiction was counsel, who on summation could argue the law as well as the facts. Most confusing of all was the court's charge. Colonial courts sat with more than one judge on the bench, each judge was free to deliver a charge if he wished to do so, and sometimes the charges of different judges were contradictory.

Second, even when a court's instructions were unanimous, judges lacked power to reject jury verdicts that did not follow the instructions. In some of the six colonies, judges could urge jurors to reconsider their verdicts, but if juries adhered to their verdicts, judges were required in all six colonies to accept them. Thus, in all six colonies, juries drawn from localities rather than judges or legislatures determined what constituted the law of those localities. As Robert Treat Paine, a Massachusetts attorney, noted initially in the late 1760s and later in the early 1770s, the "Jury ha[d] a right to do as they please[d]" and "no verdicts . . . [were] thrown out."

In New York, trial judges sitting on county courts exercised power to reject jury verdicts contrary to the law or the evidence. But county court judges were not reliable agents of the provincial government. Although they were formally appointed by the governor, they were nominated by the assembly, which almost certainly deferred, when it made nominations, to the assemblymen from the county for which judges were being nominated to serve. Because of the procedures by which appeals were taken, judges of the central, provincial court did not have power to set aside jury verdicts. In short, New York law, like the law of Maryland, New England, and New Jersey, was determined by local figures—in this instance, local jurors working under the control of local judges.

In Virginia, judges enjoyed greater control over the legal process. In ordinary cases, judges enjoyed power to reject jury verdicts that they found contrary to the law or to the evidence; on rare occasions, judges even entered judgment contrary to a verdict they had rejected without first having a new jury trial. Only in cases involving a "point of public liberty" or "in which the judges may be suspected of bias" were juries free, according to Thomas Jefferson's *Notes on Virginia*, as a matter of their own discretion, "to decide both law and fact" without judges having power to overrule them.

Still, despite the power of judges to control juries in all but politically sensitive cases, the legal system of colonial Virginia was not centralized. Local rather than central judges remained in control. Local county courts were self-perpetuating bodies: when a judge left the bench, the remaining judges nominated his successor, and, if the governor failed to appoint their nominee, the judges typically resigned en masse, thereby leaving the county without a government. Moreover, although colonial Virginia did enjoy regularized procedures for taking appeals from county courts to the colony-wide General Court, the county courts often failed to follow General Court precedents, to obey and enforce judgments of the latter court, or to execute orders of the governor. Virginia courts even nullified legislation. *Reeves v. Waller*, for example, dealt with a 1715 statute requiring suits for the collection of debts under five pounds to be brought by petition and tried without a jury rather than by writs leading to jury trials. In *Reeves*, the General Court initially nullified the statute when it upheld a jury verdict for forty shillings. Subsequent county courts then nullified *Reeves* when they set aside jury verdicts under five pounds and required plaintiffs to bring suit using the simpler petition procedure, which helped the county courts keep their dockets clear. County courts, in short, not the governor and General Court, ruled Virginia.

Central authority in the eight colonies considered so far was further weakened by the refusal of many judges to use whatever power they did possess to control juries. Instead, they often allowed juries to determine law as well as fact by refusing to give them instructions. According to one commentator who reviewed eighteenth-century Virginia practice in an 1831 brief, there were "numerous cases" in which the jury "retired without a word said by the court upon the subject" of the case. Indeed, throughout the eight colonies in which juries enjoyed varying degrees of power to determine law, judges and lawyers routinely deferred to juries.

Jury instructions everywhere were brief and rudimentary. In Massachusetts, for example, lawyers could and did assume, as did James Sullivan, a future governor of the state, in a 1779 letter to Elbridge Gerry, another future governor, that jurors were "good judges of the common law of the land." John Adams had agreed in one of his pre-Revolutionary cases that "the general Rules of Law and common Regulations of Society, under which ordinary Transactions arrange[d] themselves . . . [were] well enough known to ordinary Jurors." Accordingly, juries might be directed, as one superior court judge in fact directed them in 1759, that, as to many matters, they "need[ed] no Explanation [since] your Good Sence & understanding will Direct ye as to them."

In Connecticut, as a general practice, courts merely summarized the opposing claims without commenting on the law involved in pending cases, while in New Hampshire one judge told a jury "to do justice between the parties not by any quirks of the law . . . but by common sense as between man and man." Likewise, in one 1707 criminal case in colonial New York, the chief justice informed the jury that "there are some points [of law] I am not now prepared to answer," while in another 1741 case the court charged the jury only that "the evidence from the prosecution's witnesses seemed so ample, so full, so clear and satisfactory" that it should convict the prisoner "if you have no particular reasons in your own breast, in your consciences to discredit them." Six years earlier Chief Justice James DeLancey had similarly instructed a jury on "a matter of law, no doubt which," he said, "you *may* leave to the court," thereby implying that the jury could determine the matter of law by itself. Even in South Carolina, where juries were under total judicial control, one jury was instructed "to find a general verdict, or a special one, . . . as they thought proper," and another jury was told "to give what they thought reasonable" in "damages." In other cases, no instructions were given at all.

In short, mid-eighteenth-century juries in eight of Britain's thirteen North American colonies possessed significant power to determine the law as well as the facts of the cases they decided. Even in colonies where juries did not possess full power, judges often deferred to them and allowed them to decide the law. And when local judges did control juries, they often acted independently of central judicial control. Most important, when juries exercised power to determine the law, they sometimes used their power to nullify legislation, even acts of Parliament, and to refuse obedience to other commands of Crown authorities.

Three cases illustrate the power of juries. *Erving v. Cradock* arose in Massachusetts after a royal customs collector had seized a merchant vessel for smuggling and had had it condemned in the Vice Admiralty Court. The merchant then sued the collector at common law for damages for alleged unlawful seizure of the vessel. All five judges of the Massachusetts Superior Court charged the jury that the decree of the admiralty court was res judicata on the issue of the lawfulness of the customs collector's seizure and thus that the jury was bound to find a verdict in the collector's favor. The jury nonetheless ignored its instructions, found in favor of the merchant, and awarded damages of five hundred pounds, thereby warning the collector that he would face substantial liabilities if he continued to enforce laws against smuggling. The jury, in effect, declared Parliament's Navigation Acts null and void and rendered them of little effect.

The *Parsons' Cause* in Virginia did the same to a judgment of the Privy Council. Under legislation dating back to 1696, Virginia parishes paid clergymen of the Anglican church in tobacco at the rate of sixteen thousand pounds per year, which at a typical value of ten shillings per hundred pounds produced an income of eighty pounds sterling. But in 1758 a drought led to an increase in the price of tobacco and to a concern that ministers would be overpaid. Therefore the legislature passed what became known as the Two Penny Act, which allowed parishes to pay the clergy in cash or tobacco at a rate of two pennies per pound of tobacco. This produced an annual salary of 130 pounds sterling. When the price of tobacco in fact rose to six pence per pound, which would have given ministers a salary of nearly 400 pounds if they had been paid in tobacco at the market rate, several of them asked the Privy Council to disallow the Two Penny Act. The council did disallow the 1758 act, which led several parsons to bring suit to recover the difference between the 130 pounds salary they received and the 400 pounds salary to which they felt entitled. In the *Parsons' Cause*, a Virginia county court ruled as a matter of law that the plaintiffs were entitled to be paid at the six shillings per pound rate and summoned a jury of inquiry to determine the precise damages the plaintiffs had suffered. The jury, however, returned a nominal verdict of one shilling, which had the practical effect of nullifying both the disallowance by the Privy Council and the Virginia county court's ruling of law that the Two Penny Act did not apply.

The *Zenger* case provides the third illustration. The case arose when Governor William Cosby of New York instituted a prosecution against a local printer, John Peter Zenger, for publishing articles that, according to Cosby, constituted seditious libel. The substantive issue in the case was whether the articles amounted to a libel: the prosecution on behalf of Cosby claimed they were libelous as a matter of law, whereas Zenger's attorney claimed they were true and therefore not libelous. Zenger's attorney and the prosecutor also disagreed about who should decide that issue: the prosecutor argued that the issue should be decided by the court, whereas Zenger's counsel sought to have the jury decide the issue. Contemporary law in England supported the argument of the prosecution, but the jury took the law into its own hands, decided that truth constituted a defense, and therefore concluded that Zenger's articles did not amount to seditious libel. English law, as correctly interpreted by a Crown officer, was thereby rendered null and void.

Thus, in the eight colonies where juries had at least some degree of jurisdiction over the law, law ultimately was not what Parliament or a colonial legislature declared by statute, what an entity of the Crown decided in London, or what a royal official ruled in America. The law was what a local jury drawn from a local vicinage said it was. Decisions of local juries, in short, trumped acts of Parliament, colonial legislatures, the Privy Council, and royal officials in America.

In the five remaining colonies—Delaware, Georgia, North Carolina, Pennsylvania, and South Carolina—judges kept juries under tighter control, and as a result, judges rather than juries determined the law. However, except perhaps in Pennsylvania, law remained a local phenomenon, and local judges assumed implicit power to nullify the laws of England and the acts of their own legislatures.

Law was local in mid-eighteenth-century Delaware, Georgia, and South Carolina because all three were small colonies. Delaware remains today the second smallest state in the continental United States, and in the 1750s Georgia and South Carolina also were tiny, with settlements clustered along the coast surrounding Savannah in Georgia and Charleston in South Carolina. South Carolina was the wealthiest and most populous of the three colonies, but as late as 1750 it had only twenty-five thousand white inhabitants, which made it about as large as a midsize American town of today. The local Court of Common Pleas was able to administer the law without the help of law-finding jurors because most of the twenty-five thousand inhabitants lived in or near Charleston and had enough informal contacts with judges and lawyers to be able to influence them and be influenced by them. But when settlement began to expand inland in the 1760s and 1770s, courts in Charleston and Savannah lacked sufficient contact with the people of the interior and so proved unable to administer and enforce law there. They needed the help of jurors who, by determining applicable law, could share responsibility for the results cases reached and thereby participate in enforcing those results.

Like courts elsewhere in the thirteen colonies, those of Delaware,

Georgia, and South Carolina also felt free to question English law and legislative law. The 1760 South Carolina case of *Watson v. Williams* provides an example. At common law in England, an administrator of a decedent's estate was permitted when paying the decedent's debts to prefer some creditors over others. Thus, when the South Carolina legislature enacted a statute requiring administrators to pay all creditors equally, the statute was challenged as violative of the provision in South Carolina's charter prohibiting the enactment of laws repugnant to the laws of England. The *Watson* case accordingly put the South Carolina Court of Common Pleas in a bind: either it had to declare an act of its own legislature null and void or it had to declare that local legislation trumped the law of England. Relying on English authority, it held that it lacked power to declare the act of a coordinate branch of government—its own legislature—null and void; to exercise such power, it said, "would be for the courts jus dare & not dicere," which would leave "everything . . . to precarious & arbitrary will & pleasure." Instead, the South Carolina court invalidated the common law rule allowing administrators to prefer some creditors over others. It declared that, although its legislature could not enact laws repugnant to the laws of England, the legislature could enact legislation modifying the common law. The court ruled the South Carolina statute to be a modification rather than a rejection of the common law, and on the basis of that imprecise distinction, it left its own legislation in place and nullified the common law.

The two colonies not yet discussed—North Carolina and Pennsylvania—both were geographically large entities. In North Carolina, judges routinely set aside jury verdicts that were contrary to law or evidence, with the result that courts rather than juries retained control over the law. In addition, enabling legislation directed the North Carolina Supreme Court to sit in five different locations throughout the colony in an effort to control both juries and the lower courts in those locations. The supreme court, however, succeeded fully in controlling the law only in two eastern locations—the areas around New Bern, the colonial capital, and Edenton, the site of initial European settlement. In western North Carolina, scheduled sessions of the supreme court frequently failed to occur. County courts did meet regularly, but they conducted only local business that served the interests of local people; they did not provide forums for the assertion of creditors' claims or outsiders' property rights. Thus, the courts of North Carolina, like those of Delaware, Georgia, and South Carolina, were essentially local courts able to enforce law only in the vicinity of where they sat.

Pennsylvania was the one colony in which a central supreme court may have been able to determine the law and enforce it throughout the province. As Pennsylvania's chief justice declared in 1774, it was "a settled rule, that courts of law determine law; a jury facts. Upon which maxim," he added, "every security depends in an English country." But even in Pennsylvania there was opposition to such central judicial control. A 1772 essay took the position that "*if a jury will take upon them the knowledge of the law* . . . , *they may*" so that they could serve as "*guardian* of our legal liberties against arbitrary injustice" and protect against "judges . . . more likely to be under an influence which is injurious to the rights of the people." Pennsylvania also suffered a rebellion, that of the Paxton Boys, which it put down only by promising to grant rebel requests and pardoning the rebels for the heinous murders they had committed.

Moreover, Pennsylvania had a special form of government. It was a proprietary colony; its judges were appointed not by the Crown but by the proprietor. Those judges, in turn, felt free to nullify parliamentary statutes and rules of the common law. The supreme court held, for example, that the Statute of Frauds, enacted in 1677, did not apply in Pennsylvania. Its theory was that the statute was enacted after Charles II had granted New York, of which Pennsylvania was then a part, to his brother, the duke of York, in 1664, although the enactment took place before a subsequent grant to William Penn in 1681. The basic rule was that statutes passed before a colony's settlement were applicable, but those passed after the settlement were not.

Another parliamentary act prohibited the arrest and incarceration of soldiers and sailors in litigation brought by private parties. The supreme court held that the act did "extend to this province," but it also ordered a member of the military "committed to the custody of the sheriff of the city & county of Philadelphia" because the plaintiff's "cause of action [was] just & [could] not be determined" fairly if the defendant was not kept in jail. The court similarly ignored Parliament's legislation when, for a period of two years between 1757 and 1759, in the midst of the French and Indian War, it kept a prisoner in the Philadelphia jail and thereby prevented the military from enlisting him.

Pennsylvania judges also rejected the common law. In one case, for example, a defendant in a suit of debt on a bond offered to prove lack of consideration as a defense. The plaintiff responded that, at common law, "the consideration of a bond is not enquirable into, the passing of the bond being a gift in law." The court, however, rejected the plaintiff's argument, even though it was backed by citations to four English cases. It declared "that there being no Court of Chancery in this province," it was necessary "to prevent a failure of justice, to let the defendants in under the plea of payment to prove . . . want of consideration," which the chief justice declared "to be the constant practice of the courts of justice in this province for thirty nine years past."

Meanwhile, three young lawyers in New York—William Livingston, William Smith Jr., and John Morin Scott—were urging the colonial assembly to ignore English law. In a 1753 debate on the founding of a college for the colony, they argued in their publication, *The Independent Reflector*, that the assembly had power to charter a corporation to administer a college; in so arguing, they urged rejection of the English rule that only the Crown could issue a corporate charter. For them, the power of local institutions trumped the law of Parliament and the Crown: a local colonial assembly could treat central law as null and void and of no effect. Similarly, in the case of *Freebody v. Brenton*, which dragged on for most of the third quarter of the eighteenth century, Rhode Island's highest court followed its own "constant invariable practice" and declined to enforce a Privy Council order, urging that it functioned "under a peculiar constitution" and had a duty of "making or giving judgment" according to the "modes of practice, laws & customs" of Rhode Island—not simply giving literal obedience to the Privy Council. Here was yet another example of colonial law nullifying central law.

In view of the ability of colonial courts and juries to nullify English law and the acts of British officials, readers may be wondering whether imperial officials faced insuperable difficulties in governing the colonies. They did, in fact, face some difficulties, but for two reasons they were able to keep the difficulties under control.

First, Britain did not attempt to govern its colonies in depth. The

Crown set broad guidelines that it required colonies to follow, but at least during the first six decades of the eighteenth century it gave the colonies broad flexibility about how to apply the guidelines. Even individual counties enjoyed flexibility. For example, beginning with William III, Britain required the colonies to support and favor Protestantism. But many sorts of Protestant structures were allowed: an Anglican establishment in Virginia, a Congregational establishment in Massachusetts, a plural establishment in New York, Quaker hegemony in Pennsylvania, and disestablishment in Rhode Island. Britain also permitted Maryland to tolerate Catholics and New York City and Newport, Rhode Island, to tolerate Jews.

Likewise, beginning with Charles II, the Crown required all colonies to adopt the common law. But the speed with which individual colonies received the common law differed. It was already in place in mid-seventeenth-century Virginia, but not fully in place in Massachusetts until the mid-eighteenth century. Moreover, the common law was amorphous. It meant different things to different people, and, as a result, the law in different colonies was somewhat diverse. Fornication, for example, was punished in South Carolina only if it led to the birth of a child requiring public support. In Massachusetts, in contrast, fornication was a sin; couples were prosecuted even when they married after having had intercourse and, if witnesses to the intercourse were prepared to testify, even if no pregnancy resulted. In most of New York, fornication ceased by the mid-eighteenth century to be a matter for public prosecution at all, although men who fathered out-of-wedlock children were required to post bonds to guarantee their support. But, Suffolk County on Long Island, which had been settled by Puritan New Englanders, was an exception that followed procedures akin to Massachusetts practice.

Slavery was another subject on which the laws of the thirteen colonies differed. As Daniel Dulany wrote in 1767, "the condition of slaves in the different colonies [was] considered on various principles, established either by peculiar local laws, or dictated by the diverse genius and situation of the people." Thus, in Virginia, a master who killed a slave could be indicted for murder, although it was nearly impossible to obtain convictions for the offense. In South Carolina, in contrast, such a master would only be liable to pay a fine. South of the Mason-Dixon line, according to Dulany, slaves were treated as chattels "on the same footing with a mare or a cow." Among other things, the law did not recognize slave marriages. In Massachusetts, in contrast, slaves were regarded as human beings who possessed legal rights, including the right to marry.

And, as was shown above, a third subject on which the different colonies had different law concerned the power of judges to control the law-finding capacity of juries. There were other subjects as well. In short, British officials facilitated their governance of diverse localities, the judges and juries of which had power to nullify centrally imposed law, by giving the people of those localities freedom to choose the specific legal rules under which they would be governed.

Second, in return for freedom to choose their own law, the people of localities chose to accept most of the norms that Crown officials desired. Colonial Americans were proud members of the British Empire who understood that their own freedom and prosperity depended on the successes of the empire. They were inclined to grant imperial requests. Thus, as late as the early 1770s, in the midst of a growing constitutional crisis, the Rhode Island Superior Court in *Freebody v. Brenton* conceded its "obligation of duty and respect" to the Privy Council's "right . . . of hearing and determining all matter of appeal."

Until the 1760s, few irresolvable conflicts arose between British officials seeking to enforce central norms and colonial institutions inclined to resist them. Following policies of accommodation and compromise, both sides almost always stepped back from the precipice of ultimate coercion or resistance. But when conflict did occur and local judges or juries resisted Crown policy, as in the cases and practices discussed above, local forces typically won. We can be confident, in short, that by the middle of the eighteenth century colonial courts possessed and had frequently used power to nullify legislation and other central government commands.

CHAPTER TWO

The Consensus Community

As chapter 1 demonstrated, real power in colonial British North America lay mainly in the hands of local, usually county, courts. In some colonies, juries possessed power to determine both law and fact and thereby maintained local control of the courts; in others, local judges assumed control in conjunction with informal networks of other leading men. When local judges and juries freely nullified the legislation and other commands of central authorities, weak governors and inactive legislatures rarely interfered. Even if they had wanted to interfere, they lacked the capacity for doing so because eighteenth-century government, unlike government today, did not consist of a ubiquitous bureaucracy under the command of central political authorities.

The weakness of central institutions did not, however, mean that colonial government performed only limited functions. On the contrary, colonial government regulated its subjects' lives in pervasive detail. Local judges and juries, as vital entities of government, maintained order, adjudicated disputes, protected life and property, enforced moral values, apportioned and collected taxes, supervised the construction and maintenance of highways, issued licenses, and regulated licensees' businesses. Through administration of the Settlement Law, which permitted localities to exclude undesired newcomers, and the Poor Law, which made localities liable for the support and hence the general well-being of all who were born and raised in a locality and all newcomers who had not been excluded, the legal system fostered community self-definition and a sense of community responsibility for inhabitants. Indeed, in some colonies, the courts of general sessions of the peace, which possessed basic criminal, administrative, and some minor forms of civil jurisdiction, also performed the executive and even the legislative functions of local government.

The work of the courts, in sum, was of an undifferentiated, pervasive character. The undifferentiated character of that work was important for present purposes because it obscured distinctions between legislation, administration, and adjudication drawn by political theorists. Despite the early statement of Baron Montesquieu, the French theorist of the modern doctrine of separation of powers, Americans as late as the 1780s did not routinely distinguish the judiciary as an independent branch that exercised only "judicial" functions. They saw only "two powers in any government, viz., the power to make laws, and the power to execute them; for the judicial power is only a branch of the executive." Colonial Americans did not, that is, draw a clear distinction between law and politics.

The courts thus did not function in what we would understand as a purely legal mode. They mixed politics with law. How they did so is the core question that this chapter addresses.

Colonial courts functioned differently than modern legal and political entities because the social context in which they existed differed profoundly from the social structure of the United States today. Eighteenth-century British colonials were more tied to their families and rooted in their localities than most Americans are today; they were not free-floating individuals, like many of us, who select the other individuals with whom we will form close relationships.

Most eighteenth-century colonials did not determine in their youth what they would become as adults. Rather they were born into the economic, social, and cultural networks around which their adult lives typically would center. Most colonials were children of farmers who would themselves become farmers when they attained maturity. Few had the option, by choosing some profession other than farming, of becoming embedded in a network different from the one into which they had been born. Although they might hope to prosper, to increase their wealth, and even to obtain additional land, few could imagine, as many of us do, that they had the capacity either to change their lives or to change the world around them. No one had a conception that there was any possibility of significant social change.

Family ties bound individuals to their neighborhood. Consider, for example, Elizabeth Montague of Middlesex County, Virginia, who at the time of her death was related by blood or marriage to three-fourths of the households in the county. Family connections such as those enjoyed by Montague provided an individual with invaluable support in times of crisis and stress, such as impoverishment, illness, violent onslaught, or even death in the immediate family. At a time when government, market, and charitable institutions such as police, hospitals, doctors, schools, and welfare agencies were weak or nonexistent, a person's ties to family were often the only means that could save her from standing helpless and alone in the wilderness in times of trouble. Family ties were so important that many people, especially children, elderly people, and single women, dared not leave a community where they had ties and move to one where they would dwell in isolation.

Ties to family and neighbors also had another impact: they deprived people of privacy and anonymity. In neighborhoods where everyone was known, there could be no secrets and no anonymous misbehavior. If a person broke the neighborhood's moral code or failed to perform a duty that the community required, gossip would promptly spread news of the breach or failure to everyone. A youth's parents, family, and neighbors, like the all-knowing God, learned of every one of his peccadillos.

Societal realities such as these determined the scope and design of law and government. Once they had been established, local communities tended to become simply ongoing. Since no one had a clear concept of the possibility of social change, no one imagined that the judges who governed communities possessed policy-making prerogatives of the sort that we assume Congress and the president possess today. Since no one had a clear concept of the possibility of social change, colonials did not conceive of law or even politics as an instrument of change. It was a commonplace, as chief justice and future loyalist governor, Thomas Hutchinson of Massachusetts, informed a grand jury in 1769, that those who "execut[ed] the Law . . . [ought] not to enquire into . . . [its] Reason and Policy," but ought merely "to enquire what is Law."

Daniel Dulany, an early thinker from Maryland, agreed in 1728 that courts merely dispensed justice according to law, which was thought to be "*founded in principles, that are permanent,* uniform *and* universal." It was vital, as Hutchinson said in other grand jury charges in the late 1760s, that "the Laws of every State ought always to be fixed, [and] certain" and that "*the Judge should never be the Legislator*:

Because, then the Will of the Judge would be the Law: and this tends to a State of Slavery." A young lawyer who would oppose Hutchinson in the War for Independence and ultimately would become the second president of the United States, John Adams, wrote at approximately the same time as Hutchinson was delivering his charges that "every possible Case" ought to be "settled in a Precedent leav[ing] nothing, or but little to the arbitrary Will or uninformed Reason of Prince or Judge."

The chief executive of each colony—the governor—similarly was thought to have no power to make policy. The same was true for the chief executive of the realm—the king—who by the mid-eighteenth century possessed little real power. Some colonials even had doubts about the power of the legislature to enact laws. Even before the late eighteenth-century adoption of written constitutions, arguments were being made, in the words of a 1775 New York pamphlet, that "something must exist in a free state, which no part of it can be authorised to alter or destroy."

To understand what enabled colonials to hold such views, we need to focus on what has already been mentioned above—that the eighteenth century was a time when few people imagined that social change was possible and nearly everyone assumed that life would go on essentially as it had for decades. Society was seen as a stable organism that grew and maintained itself of its own accord.

It followed from this view of society that no one in government needed to make policy choices about the direction that law, government, and the society ought to take. Of course, bad people might threaten the health and stability of the organism: foreign monarchs often threatened destruction of the organism by war, and criminals and other evil people posed menaces to peace and stability at home. The king had the duty to make the decisions needed to protect the realm from foreign threats, and his judges and juries performed the task of doing justice to malefactors at home. But doing justice did not entail either policy choice or coercion of the good people of a community; on the contrary, courts worked harmoniously with those people to protect and defend the values embedded within the common law of property, stability, and morality that most people of the community took for granted.

Courts and community worked together; they lacked power to do otherwise. Although judges of colonial common law courts theoretically were appointed by the governor and their commissions typically ran only during pleasure, the judges, once appointed, were quite free from the influence of the Crown. In contrast, their freedom from the lower house of the legislature, collectively the representative of local communities, was much more in doubt, given that the legislatures controlled the judges' salaries.

Above all, judges, like juries, were part of the community from which they came. Nearly all judges were drawn not from the lower reaches of the English bureaucracy, but rather were men of local prominence. The key to becoming a judge was not that one was a lawyer, for nearly all colonial judges were not, but that one was a man of substance who commanded the respect of his community. Men who had obtained place in part because they possessed the trust and confidence of their fellow subjects would not lightly violate that trust. Although they were appointed by the Crown, judges usually sought to retain the confidence and respect of their local communities and hence would be unlikely to reject legal traditions that were widely esteemed in their community.

Even in colonies where judges could overrule juries and thus theoretically had power to reject community standards, it is doubtful whether they could have enforced their judgments if they routinely had tried to do so. The crucial fact about government in mid-eighteenth-century America was that subordinate officials like sheriffs, deputy sheriffs, and constables—the men with legal responsibility for enforcing judgments—could do so only when local communities were willing to permit judgments to be enforced. The difficulty was not merely that subordinate officials were liable to suits for damages, for that liability could have been judicially limited. A greater difficulty lay in the Anglo-American tradition of government—a tradition with roots in the Middle Ages and still very much alive in the eighteenth-century British colonial world. In that tradition, government did not have vast bureaucratic armies of officials to enforce its laws, but instead relied on its subjects to aid in their task of law enforcement the few officials who did exist.

The ultimate difficulty was that officials simply lacked effective power to coerce people to obey the law. Coercive use of violence by government simply could not bring victory in eighteenth-century

America over recalcitrant individuals who had supporters in their community. If an official failed by himself to coerce a recalcitrant person, he could not call for the aid of a substantial body of force other than fellow members of the community, organized as the militia; if the militia was on the side of the recalcitrant person, it would not, of course, aid the official. Thus, the only way for officials to ensure enforcement of the law was to obtain local community support for the law, and the best way to obtain that support was to permit local communities to determine the substance of the law, either through legal institutions such as the jury or through informal networks such as those in South Carolina.

The ability of courts to govern through juries and other informal networks was deeply dependent, in turn, on the fixed and certain nature of the law. If law had been uncertain and individual jurors had manifested differing opinions about its substance, it would have been impossible, for instance, for jurors to have decided cases after receiving rudimentary or conflicting instructions, or even no instructions at all. The law-finding power of juries suggests ineluctably that jurors came to court with shared preconceptions about the substance of the law.

This point was explicitly made in the 1788 Connecticut case of *Pettis v. Warren*. In a black slave's suit for freedom, one juror was challenged for having a preexisting opinion "that no negro, by the laws of this state, could be holden a slave." Affirming the trial court's overruling of the challenge, the Connecticut Supreme Court held that "an opinion formed and declared upon a general principle of law, does not disqualify a juror to sit in a cause in which that principle applies." Indeed, the court observed that the jurors in every case could "all be challenged on one side or the other, if having an opinion of the law in the case is ground of challenge," since, as John Adams had noted some two decades earlier, "the general Rules of Law and common Regulations of Society . . . [were] well enough known to ordinary Jurors." Jurors, the Connecticut court believed, were "supposed to have opinions of what the law is," since they sat as "judges of law as well as fact."

One might infer further that jurors came to the court with similar preconceptions about the law, at least as it applied to disputes that frequently came before them. Indeed, one cannot escape this inference without abandoning all efforts to understand how eighteenth-century government functioned. If jurors came to court with different and possibly conflicting opinions about substantive law, one would expect to find first, that juries had difficulty reaching unanimous verdicts and that mistrials due to hung juries were correspondingly frequent, and second, that different juries at different times would reach different, perhaps inconsistent, verdicts, thereby making the law so uncertain and unpredictable that people could not plan their affairs.

In fact, no such evidence exists. On the contrary, the available evidence suggests that juries had so little difficulty reaching verdicts that they often heard and decided several cases a day. No one in the mid-eighteenth century complained about the inconsistency of jury verdicts, and as soon as such complaints were heard in the century's last decade, the system of jury law-finding began to disintegrate.

Although we have no direct evidence, most subjects probably did not desire to serve as jurors. At a time of difficult travel, few people would have cared to attend court sessions, and those who did probably were pursuing business interests from which jury duty was an unwelcome distraction. In short, there is every reason to think that eighteenth-century subjects avoided jury duty as eagerly as citizens today and that the chore was therefore distributed among as much of the eligible population as could be conscripted. Although some groups (notably women, blacks, servants, religious dissenters, and anyone who did not own land or pay taxes) may have been systematically excluded from juries, it does not seem unreasonable to infer that juries contained a random and representative cross section of the remaining population.

That conclusion suggests a final inference. If juries in fact mirrored the white, male, landholding, and taxpaying population, and if upon coming to court nearly all jurors shared similar ideas about the substance of the law, then perhaps a body of shared ideas about law permeated a large segment of the population of every territory over which a court that sat with a jury had jurisdiction. Colonial government may have been able to derive policies from and otherwise function on the basis of those shared values. Likewise, in colonies like South Carolina, where informal networks maintained links between judges and the rest of the colonial community, a set of widely shared and largely unchanging values also constituted the foundation for the community's legal system.

Those who have lived amid the twenty-first-century cacophony of conflicting interests may find it difficult to imagine how a government acting on the basis of established, unchanging norms and in the absence of serious conflict about those norms could ever function effectively. The eighteenth-century Anglo-American world, however, was sufficiently different from our own so that government in that era could have so functioned.

Several differences should be noted. First, the colonial economy was much less productive than is the economy today. As a result, less money was available for government, and most communities could afford only a few salaried officeholders. Indeed, many people did not have enough wealth and time even to participate in elections "without manifest injury to their crops."

Competition for local leadership positions also was understandably slight, and local governments lacked substantial salaried bureaucracies that could enforce decisions. Part-time police officials such as deputy sheriffs and constables enforced government decisions, so long, that is, as they did not contravene the wishes of neighbors with whom they had close economic and social ties. The ultimate enforcement body was the militia, which, as seen above, typically would not act against the community's wishes. Colonial economic conditions, in short, reduced conflict and competition in local politics and precluded the rise of coercive institutions that might have been used by one portion of a community seeking to promote its interests at the expense of others.

Second, colonial American communities differed tremendously. Religion remained important in eighteenth-century life, and America provided room for many different religious groups. Religious differences were not the only ones among the communities. Important economic differences also existed, for while most communities were agricultural, a few were either mercantile or chiefly engaged in fishing. Finally, differences in lifestyle and ambience distinguished communities, as any visitor to the restored colonial towns of Sturbridge, Massachusetts, and Williamsburg, Virginia, can see, or as any reader of the diaries of eighteenth-century travelers like Dr. Alexander Hamilton can learn.

Colonial men and families who found it important to change their residence from one community to another were able to do so. Benjamin Franklin, the foremost American of the mid-eighteenth century, had moved as an adult male from Boston to Philadelphia with relative ease, for instance, while thousands of other men, often accompanied by their families, found the move from established towns to the frontier not at all insuperable. As a result, many colonials who dissented from their own community's conception of right and justice could move without great difficulty to a more congenial community. Newly arriving immigrants were also able to identify and settle in communities that welcomed their religious beliefs, lifestyles, and economic skills. The tendency of people to live in communities they found congenial was important, particularly because it enabled communities to retain their identity by facilitating the departure of those whose personal ethical codes would have diluted that identity.

But while colonial American men could readily move between communities, they generally seem not to have established the kind of sustained intercommunity contact likely to produce conflict. American communities had long since abandoned schemes of subjugating each other or seizing each other's wealth; the Dutch of Manhattan and the Puritans of Long Island, for example, learned how to coexist when they each abandoned thoughts of conquest and developed their primary social and economic communication with their respective compatriots in the Hudson Valley and in New England rather than with each other. The availability of land, which made territorial quarrels unnecessary, and the lack of a developed transportation and communication network, which made sustained contact difficult, also help account for the infrequency of disputes between communities. Geographically proximate communities were thus able to remain distinct; to pursue their own, largely unchanging, conception of right; and to avoid intercommunity disputes that legal institutions dependent on local community support would have been incapable of resolving.

Finally, colonial politics existed within an established constitutional structure that colonials could not control. Parliament, in which colonials had no direct voice, alone possessed the power to decide many fundamental social and economic issues, and for the first sixty years of the eighteenth century it was willing to abide by decisions reached in the preceding century that often were favorable to the colonies. Thus, much of the grist for genuine political conflict was removed from the realm of imperial politics; absent a radical re-structuring of the Anglo-American system, there was simply no point in building a political organization around the issue whether, for example, Anglicans would be tolerated in Massachusetts or whether Americans would be free to trade with French Canada without restriction.

Provincial politics were not radically different. Colonial legislatures were under American control, but they could not effectively enact legislation that significantly altered the structure of colonial society since such legislation would almost always be vetoed by a colonial governor or by London. As a result, colonial legislation usually consisted of mere administration: raising and appropriating small amounts of tax money, distributing even smaller amounts of government largess, and legislating as necessary to keep the few governmental institutions functioning.

While provincial political conflict commonly occurred, it rarely involved important social issues. Of course, occasional conflicts grew from religious differences, such as the division in Pennsylvania politics between Quaker and anti-Quaker parties, and from the rivalry between seaboard and backcountry areas, such as the 1740s land-bank dispute in Massachusetts and the 1760s Regulator Movement in the Carolinas. But since these disputes could not be locally resolved within the British power structure, they quickly degenerated into mere personal and factional conflicts between leaders seeking personal advancement. Provincial political conflict may have been widespread, but as shrewdly observant colonial political writers vehemently announced, it departed from the ideal polity of consensus—a polity that may have existed in many eighteenth-century local communities.

Taken together, these facts helped to sustain a political order in colonial America radically different from the political order of America today. The stable imperial constitution combined with the penury of colonial economies and the largely unchanging character of most colonial communities to remove most social and economic issues from imperial and provincial politics. Before independence, most newly arising socioeconomic conflicts were resolved and new socio-economic decisions taken at the local level.

The penury of colonial economies had another influence: by

keeping the social elite small and depriving it of effective military and bureaucratic power necessary to coerce the people at large, the political economy of British North America denied colonial leaders the opportunity to exploit their localities in their own self-interest. Leaders generally had to govern and resolve social tensions according to values widely accepted in their localities. Finally, the real differences between localities and the capacity of many to move either alone or with their families to a community whose values they shared preserved each community's distinct identity.

As a result, the colonial American polity may, on the whole, have consisted of a series of local communities whose inhabitants collectively strove to elaborate fixed standards of right and justice and to govern their communities by those standards. Of course, they did not always succeed. As many historians have shown, a communitarian social order had at least partially broken down by the time of the American Revolution, when social conflict and tension had become endemic. Perhaps the breakdown even contributed to the Revolution. Moreover, many people—notably, African American slaves, Native Americans, women, and landless white men—were not even part of the political community, and tensions between them and the landowning white males who did constitute the community were ever present. Historians also have pointed to a good deal of conflict within the white, male, landowning community.

Nonetheless, the structure of colonial government was such that it could function effectively only in jurisdictions with some degree of consensus and shared, fixed values. When societal conflict escalated, colonial government became ineffective, as it did in many places during the decade leading up to the Revolution. Government broke down and violent conflict ensued with some frequency in the second half of the eighteenth century precisely because government had few mechanisms other than the maintenance of consensus with which to obtain obedience to its mandates. Government based upon shared values may have functioned in eighteenth-century America with only a minimal degree of effectiveness, but no other style of government was capable of functioning at all.

With this, we come to the most important point for purposes of this book: that a consensus style of government on the basis of established, unchanging values was known to most mid-eighteenth-century white, male Americans on a routine, day-to-day basis.] An individual litigant, a special-interest group, a high provincial official, even a judge, often could elicit a particular court decision or attain a long-term policy only if he could persuade the cross section of the community that acted as judges and jurors to accept the policy, and such attempts at persuasion must almost invariably have required appeals to established values he and the judges and jurors already shared. There was normally no other way to proceed.

Of course, lawyers, judges, officials, and litigants did not always find common values that could support decisions. They may often have failed, and their failures may have sensitized them to the instability inherent in processes of government by consensus. Nevertheless, the mid-eighteenth-century statesman typically was compelled to govern, the lawyer was required to practice, and the litigant was forced to argue, by molding and appealing to a consensus of largely unchanging shared values. It was in this style of government and legal practice that James Otis, John Marshall, and other statesmen, judges, and lawyers who would develop the doctrine of judicial review first learned the workings of their profession.

CHAPTER THREE

James Otis and the *Writs of Assistance Case*

Chapter 1 examined eighteenth-century cases in which local courts and juries invalidated parliamentary and other legislation and nullified decisions of the Privy Council and other royal officials. Today the Supreme Court of the United States together with lower courts has power to declare legislation unconstitutional and to decline on constitutional grounds to enforce actions taken by the executive branch. Is there a relationship between the eighteenth-century nullification cases and the power of judicial review that courts exercise today? Is there a bridge between nullification and unconstitutionality? This chapter suggests that there is such a bridge—the argument of James Otis Jr. in the 1761 Massachusetts *Writs of Assistance Case.*

Otis's argument is the first known instance in which an American court was urged to refuse to enforce legislation not on the ground that widely accepted, well-established local law trumped the wishes of central authorities but on the ground that a law adopted by a legislature violated peoples' rights. Chapter 1 discussed three cases in which the Pennsylvania Supreme Court had refused to apply parliamentary statutes, but in two of those cases the court upheld the validity of the statutes as a general matter and offered narrow reasons for not applying them to pending cases, and in the third case, the court simply ignored the legislation without giving any reason for doing so. New York's mid-eighteenth-century *Independent Reflector* had never claimed that acts of Parliament could be totally null and void, but had argued only that the New York assembly had power to charter a college—an act that common law declared to be the prerogative of the king. A South Carolina lawyer had made an argument somewhat analogous to that of Otis a year before Otis did, but the South Carolina Court of Common Pleas had rejected it. Perhaps some court somewhere may have adopted an argument such as Otis's, but, if so, no record has survived.

Otis's argument constitutes the bridge between eighteenth-century nullification practice and modern judicial review because the argument entered the public record. The Boston press published an article about the case shortly after Otis made his argument. John Adams repeated the argument four years later, and fifty-five years later he still attributed great significance to it. Most important, Otis elaborated the argument in a widely circulated pamphlet, *The Rights of the British Colonies Asserted and Proved*, that he published three years after he first made it. Otis thereby translated a constitutional practice that judges, lawyers, and juries had used with little public notice in individual cases into a publicly accessible constitutional norm. Although the court before which he argued the norm rejected his position, his argument made the position publicly available for acceptance by future courts and lawyers.

Writs of assistance, which functioned as general search warrants, had been used in Massachusetts since the 1750s. A writ of assistance authorized the surveyor of customs, with the assistance of a local officer of the peace such as a constable, in the daytime to search any house or other building in which he suspected unlawfully imported goods to be located and to seize any unlawful goods that he found. A writ of assistance, which remained in force from the date of its issuance until six months after the death of the sovereign in whose name it had been issued, authorized the customs surveyor to engage in as many searches as he deemed were needed. He did not need to make any application to anyone to conduct a search, he did not need to have probable cause before making a search, and he did not need to make any return to a court after completing a search. Issuance of a writ of assistance thus gave a customs surveyor open-ended authority for as long as he remained in office to search wherever his suspicions led, however unsupported those suspicions might be.

Six months after the death of George II in 1760, all extant writs of assistance expired. Charles Paxton, the surveyor of customs in Boston, accordingly applied to the Superior Court of Judicature for a new writ in a proceeding that became entitled *Paxton's Case*. Under the provisions of a 1696 act of Parliament, it appeared that Paxton was entitled to the writ. Several Boston merchants opposed his application, however, and they retained James Otis Jr. and Oxenbridge Thacher, a leading senior member of the Boston bar, to represent them.

Thacher argued that the 1696 statute gave power only to a court of exchequer to grant a writ of assistance, that the Massachusetts Superior Court had the jurisdiction only of the Courts of King's Bench and Common Pleas, and therefore that it had no jurisdiction to issue a writ. It was a sensible argument solidly grounded on the 1696 English legislation authorizing the issuance of writs of assistance and on the Massachusetts legislation that had created the superior court. It was not an argument of significance outside the confines of Massachusetts. If the superior court had accepted it, the argument would have disposed of the case, no writ would have been granted, and the need for writs could have been accommodated by amending either the 1696 English legislation or Massachusetts' jurisdictional legislation.

The court had to reach Otis's argument on the merits of whether Paxton was entitled to a writ only if it rejected Thacher's jurisdictional claim. But because the 1696 act of Parliament clearly entitled Paxton to the writ as long as the superior court had jurisdiction to issue it, Otis had a difficult mountain to climb. Unable to construe the act in his clients' favor, Otis urged the superior court to do what Massachusetts courts and juries, along with courts and juries elsewhere in America, had long been doing—to refuse to apply the act. He called it an act against the constitution.

John Adams, who attended the hearing as a young lawyer, made contemporaneous notes. According to those notes, Otis began:

This Writ is against the Fundamental Principles of Law. The Privilege of House. A Man, who is quiet, is as secure in his House, as a Prince in his Castle. . . .

All Precedents and this am'g the Rest are under the Control of the Principles of Law. Ld. Talbot. Better to observe the known Principles of Law thn any one Precedent, tho in the House of Lords.—

As to Acts of Parliament, An Act against the Constitution is void: an Act against natural Equity is void: and if an Act of Parliament should be made, in the very Words of this Petition, it would be void. The Executive Courts must pass such Acts into disuse—

8 Rep. 118. from Viner.—Reason of the Com Law to control an Act of Parliament.

Otis's citation of 8 Rep. 118 was to *Dr. Bonham's Case*, which Sir Edward Coke had decided in 1610. The case had arisen when the Royal College of Physicians, on which Parliament had conferred extensive power to govern the practice of medicine in London, prosecuted Dr. Bonham, adjudged him to be in violation of its rules, and then fined and imprisoned him. When Bonham brought a suit for false imprisonment, Coke decided in his favor on the ground that, in both prosecuting and adjudicating Bonham's case, the College of Physicians had violated the common law maxim that a man may not be judge in his own case. To the college's rejoinder that Parliament had authorized it to be both prosecutor and judge, Coke proclaimed the following dictum:

> It appears in our books, that in many cases the common law will controul Acts of Parliament, and sometimes adjudge them to be utterly void, for when an Act of Parliament is against common right and reason, or repugnant, or impossible to be performed, the common law will controul it, and adjudge such Act to be void.

On its face, Coke's dictum is ambiguous: it is not clear whether he invalidated the parliamentary statute because it violated what he called "common right"—an approach that would be akin to modern judicial review, which voids legislation that is inconsistent with fundamental constitutional principles, or whether he refused to apply the statute in the manner requested by the College of Physicians because it was repugnant or incapable of being performed consistently with its own terms—an approach that would be akin to statutory construction, where judges try to make sense out of ambiguous, possibly even inconsistent, legislation by interpreting it in light of established background common law principles. Judges must inevitably engage in the task of statutory construction, since legislative acts will always contain some ambiguity, and statutory construction does not threaten legislative supremacy, because a legislature can always overrule a court's constructional decision by reenacting its statute in unambiguous terms.

English cases in the century and a half after *Bonham's Case* increasingly read it as a statutory construction case, and Blackstone, in his *Commentaries on the Laws of England*, published in the 1760s after the *Writs of Assistance Case* had been decided, left no doubt that Parliament was supreme and that judges could not invalidate or otherwise refuse to apply legislation that they found contrary to common right. The weight of modern scholarship agrees that *Bonham's Case* was about statutory construction, not unconstitutionality, and thus that Otis misunderstood Coke's words.

Otis, however, could not have been aware of the commentary of modern scholars and may not have known the views of his contemporaries in England. What he did know was how Massachusetts juries treated acts of Parliament and determinations of other British officials when those acts trespassed on colonial rights; the jurors of Massachusetts passed those acts and determinations into disuse. Otis also may have known of other American courts and juries that behaved in the same way. He surely understood that law for Americans was not the enactment of some distant legislature or the directive of some distant bureaucrat; law was a set of norms consistent with an understanding of constitutionalism acceptable to local people. Read in the context of that understanding—of Otis's understanding—*Bonham's Case* meant what Otis said it meant: that an act of Parliament inconsistent with the constitution, as Americans knew the constitution, was null and void and of no force in America and that the practice of colonial courts was to pass such an act into disuse and render it of no effect.

Otis's argument about the unconstitutionality of the act authorizing writs of assistance may have been inconsistent with the true meaning of *Bonham's Case*, but it was not inconsistent with American precedent. Just one year earlier, a South Carolina attorney had argued in *Watson v. Williams*, which was analyzed in chapter 1, that the act of the South Carolina legislature requiring administrators to treat all creditors equally violated South Carolina's charter and was therefore unconstitutional, null and void, and of no effect. The South Carolina Court of Common Pleas rejected his argument and upheld the statute, just as the Massachusetts Superior Court rejected Otis's argument. But the South Carolina court in the process had held that the common law rule allowing administrators to favor some creditors over others was null, void, and of no effect in the colony. The South Carolina court, that is, ruled as New York's mid-century *Independent Reflector* would have had it rule—it held that local legislatively enacted law had priority over distantly created imperial law. That was, in essence, what Otis was asking the Massachusetts Superior Court to do in the *Writs of Assistance Case.*

Of course, Otis asked the Massachusetts court to take an extreme step that the South Carolina court had not been asked to take. In *Watson v. Williams*, the colonial South Carolina court was asked only to consider the constitutionality of an act of a colonial legislature— an act of a coordinate branch of government. In the *Writs of Assistance Case*, Otis asked the Massachusetts Superior Court to invalidate an act of the High Court of Parliament, which was understood to be the highest court in the realm. He was asking a court that was lower in the hierarchical chain of jurisdiction to disobey a court at the top of the chain. That, however, was again analogous to what New York's mid-eighteenth-century lawyers had urged, what Pennsylvania's Supreme Court on several occasions had done, and what Virginia county courts did with some frequency.

In short, the *Writs of Assistance Case* was not unprecedented. It did not break new ground. The case was unique and important because of the publicity it received, largely through the hands of Otis himself.

Thus, an article about the *Writs of Assistance Case* appeared in the *Boston Gazette* on November 23, 1761, shortly after the case was decided. Although Otis's argument was not summarized in the article, it is likely that some Bostonians were aware of it. But it is unclear how widespread knowledge of his argument was, and it is also unclear how widely knowledge of the *Writs of Assistants Case* spread to other colonies.

Otis made up for whatever lack of widespread knowledge there may have been, however, with his 1764 pamphlet, *The Rights of the British Colonies Asserted and Proved.* This pamphlet was published along with a memorial written by Otis on behalf of Boston's representatives to the Massachusetts General Court, which, in turn, forwarded the memorial to the colony's agent in London. The pamphlet together with the memorial was reprinted in London as well as three more times in the colonies before the Stamp Act crisis, to which the next chapter will turn, was over.

The argument that Otis had made in the *Writs of Assistance Case* was repeated in two places in the pamphlet and once in the memorial. He began by declaring the

> power of Parliament . . . [is] uncontrollable but by themselves, and we must obey. They only can repeal their own acts. There would be an end of all government if one or a number of subjects or subordinate provinces should take upon them so far to judge of the justice of an act of Parliament as to refuse obedience to it. . . . Therefore let Parliament lay what burdens they please on us, we must, it is our duty to submit and patiently bear them till they will be pleased to relieve us.

Note how this quoted passage rejects the traditional practice of localities refusing to obey acts of central authorities. The people's hands, in Otis's view, were "tied by the passage of an act of Parliament," but their "mouths [were] not stopped." Otis continued:

> I take it every subject has a right to give his sentiments to the public. . . . Reasons may be given why an act ought to be repealed, and yet obedience must be yielded to it till that repeal takes place. If the reasons that can be given against an act are such as plainly demonstrate that it is against *natural* equity, the executive courts will adjudge such acts void. It may be questioned by some, though I make no doubt of it, whether they are not obliged by their oaths to adjudge such act void. If there is not a right of private judgment to be exercised, so far at least as to petition for a repeal or to determine the expediency of risking a trial at law, Parliament might make itself arbitrary, which it is conceived it cannot by the constitution.

Otis made the same argument—that subjects must obey an unconstitutional law although courts had the power and duty to invalidate it—later in the pamphlet.

> To say that Parliament is absolute and arbitrary is a contradiction. The Parliament cannot make 2 and 2, 5; omnipotency cannot do it. The supreme power in a state is *jus dicere* only; *jus dare*, strictly

speaking, belongs only to GOD. Parliaments are in all cases to *declare* what is for the good of the whole, but it is not the *declaration* of Parliament that makes it so. There must be in every instance a higher authority, viz., GOD. Should an act of Parliament be against any of *his* natural laws, which are *immutably* true, *their* declaration would be contrary to eternal truth, equity, and justice, and consequently void: and so it would be adjudged by Parliament itself when convinced of their mistake. . . . When such a mistake is evident and palpable . . . , the judges of the executive courts have declared the act "of a whole Parliament void." See here the grandeur of the British constitution! . . . The supreme *legislative* and the supreme *executive* are a perpetual check and balance to each other. If the supreme legislative errs it is informed by the supreme executive in the King's courts of law. . . . This is government! This is a constitution!

The memorial of Boston's representatives to the general court was even clearer:

The power of the British Parliament is held as sacred and as uncontrollable in the colonies as in England. The question is not upon the general power or right of the Parliament, but whether it is not circumscribed within some equitable and reasonable bounds. 'Tis hoped it will not be considered as a new doctrine that even the authority of the Parliament of *Great Britain* is circumscribed by certain bounds which if exceeded their acts become those of mere *power* without *right*, and consequently void. The judges of England have declared in favor of these sentiments when they expressly declare that *acts of Parliament against natural equity are void.* That *acts against the fundamental principles of the British constitution are void.* This doctrine is agreeable to the law of nature and nations, and to the divine dictates of natural and revealed religion. It is contrary to reason that the supreme power should have right to alter the constitution. This would imply . . . that those who are invested with power to protect the people and support their rights and liberties have a right to make slaves of them. This is not very remote from a flat contradiction.

Taken together, these quoted passages from *The Rights of the British Colonies Asserted and Proved* offer a clear statement of the American doctrine of judicial review of the constitutionality of legislation. According to these passages, people and government entities are required to obey legislative enactments even when they disagree with their substance. But if those enactments violate either fundamental law or principles of the constitution, either the people or their entities can petition the courts to invalidate them. Ordinary courts of justice have both the power and the duty to declare unconstitutional enactments null, void, and of no effect, with the result that, after those enactments have been invalidated, they no longer need to be obeyed.

In short, the doctrine of judicial review was announced broadly to the colonial public and legal profession in 1764 and became available for use. And, as the next chapter will show, it would gain wide use during the Stamp Act crisis of the next two years. That does not mean, however, that Otis's position was politically dominant; indeed, at the start, his argument was a marginal one presented by a young lawyer to a court that rejected it.

Two competing views enjoyed predominance. The first was parliamentary or legislative sovereignty—the concept that Parliament or any other sovereign legislature, even if it is under the control of a limited set of interests rather than fully representative, can govern a society however it wants and that all people, even victims of discrimination, are obligated to obey. In view of the fact that the same interest groups, through such devices as lobbying and malapportionment, typically retain control of legislative bodies for extended periods of time, legislative sovereignty often displays a reactionary cast. But legislative sovereignty can become a vehicle of radical change if different political interests obtain dominance in the legislature.

The second competing view was popular constitutionalism—the idea that the people themselves pass on the constitutionality of law and are free to disobey whatever law they find unconstitutional. Larry Kramer, for one, has argued that early judicial review of the sort advanced by Otis was merely a tributary of popular constitutionalism, whereby judges acted in the same fashion as ordinary subjects acted, considered the constitutionality of a law in the same political way that ordinary subjects considered it, and decided issues before them on the basis of what they concluded. But for Otis, as will be seen, judicial review was quite different. Popular constitutionalism is a radical—indeed, a revolutionary—concept. Like all forms of populism, it can be driven by whatever captures the people's fancy, from the most noble ideals to the meanest prejudices. Popular constitutionalism can rapidly turn the world upside down, for good or for evil.

From the perspective of the twenty-first century, choosing among legislative supremacy, popular constitutionalism, and judicial review is eminently political in nature. Because of their political and potentially revolutionary character, however, Otis rejected both parliamentary sovereignty and popular constitutionalism. In arguing that legislation authorizing the issuance of writs of assistance was unconstitutional and void, he rejected parliamentary supremacy. In arguing that the people had to obey parliamentary legislation until a court invalidated it, he rejected popular constitutionalism. Otis favored judicial review precisely because, in his view, it was not political and because it could not, as he understood it, produce dramatic social change. When he articulated the doctrine of judicial review in *The Rights of the British Colonies*, he argued not that he was creating something new and malleable; rather he claimed he was arguing for something old and unchanging. His contention was that legislation "contrary to eternal truth, equity, and justice" was void, not because it adopted bad policy, but because "the supreme power in a state . . . [was] *jus dicere* only . . . [, while] *jus dare*, strictly speaking, belong[ed] only to God." Judicial review, according to Otis, was not political, but was governed by ongoing, fixed principles of law—longstanding norms by which courts had governed society over time. Like the colonial worldview that understood society as an ongoing enterprise incapable of fundamental change, Otis's understanding of judicial review was deeply conservative, allowing at most for gradual change and then only for change at the margins.

CHAPTER FOUR

The Stamp Act
and the Townshend Act

The patterns of accommodation and compromise through which Britain and its American colonies related to each other through the first half of the eighteenth century received a serious jolt when in 1765 Parliament adopted the Stamp Act. The act provided that documents required for clearing ships from harbors, deeds and other documents used in land grants, debt instruments and certain sorts of contracts, papers filed in court, and pamphlets and newspapers be printed or written on stamped paper that could be purchased only from royal officials whose purpose in selling the stamped paper was to collect revenue for the Crown. Americans vehemently opposed Parliament's imposition of this stamp tax.

Popular constitutionalism immediately came into play. Polemicists quickly produced a vast literature contending that the Stamp Act was unconstitutional. In Boston and Newport, Rhode Island, mobs rioted and destroyed property to force the men who had been appointed to distribute the stamped paper to resign. The threat of riots elsewhere from New Hampshire to Georgia forced all other stamp distributors to resign or to flee from the colony for which they had been appointed. As a result, no one was willing or able to put the Stamp Act into execution in Britain's thirteen mainland American colonies. The people had rendered the act unconstitutional and unenforceable.

The unconstitutionality of the act also emerged in the courts. The specific issue that confronted courts was whether to remain open and process pleas and other documents filed on unstamped paper or to close until stamps became available. On the one hand, it was urged that processing unstamped documents would violate the act of Parliament. A number of arguments were presented, on the other hand, in support of the courts' remaining open. The need to uphold law

{ 45 }

and order by maintaining the visibility of courts was one. Another was that Parliament never intended to close the courts and that, because all stamp distributors had either fled or resigned and stamps were unavailable, remaining open would not violate the intent of Parliament.

But the main argument in support of remaining open was the unconstitutionality of the Stamp Act. James Otis's pamphlet on *The Rights of the British Colonies Asserted and Proved* had been widely circulated in the previous year, and the argument about constitutionality was present on its face. A law against the constitution and natural equity that violated the fundamental rights of Englishmen, according to Otis, was null and void and of no effect. Courts were obligated to put such a law into disuse. It followed that, because the Stamp Act impeded the right of access to the courts—a right of fundamental constitutional magnitude—the requirement of filing court documents on stamped paper was unconstitutional.

Lawyers up and down the Atlantic coast advanced this argument during the fall, winter, and spring of 1765–1766. Some courts rejected the argument. But others accepted it, challenged the power of Parliament by ruling its act unconstitutional and therefore void, and thereupon remained open for business without stamped paper. And every court that accepted the argument made the argument less marginal and brought it increasingly into the mainstream of American constitutional thinking.

The Court of Common Pleas and the Probate Court of Suffolk County, Massachusetts, which sat in Boston, were among the first to remain open, with the court of common pleas holding its scheduled regular session in January 1766. The Governor's Council, after hearing arguments from John Adams that the Stamp Act was "utterly void, and of no binding force upon us" and from James Otis "that there are limits, beyond which if Parliaments go, their acts bind not," had left the decision whether to remain open in the hands of the courts themselves, which, in consultation with the Boston town meeting and in an apparent challenge to the power of Parliament, chose to remain open.

When the Massachusetts House of Representatives met later in the same month, it took the same approach and adopted a resolution, by a vote of 81 to 5, directing all courts, especially the superior court, to remain open. The council declined to concur, but it inquired whether the justices of the superior court would hold their regular session in March. The justices responded that they would hear cases if "circumstances" remained unchanged, and the court did, in fact, hear a case at its March session that had been filed before the effective date of the Stamp Act and had been continued to a future court session. By that time, rumors of the act's repeal were already circulating, and other pending business and new business were postponed. Meanwhile, all lower courts were open for business.

Rhode Island was a second colony that kept all its courts open without interruption throughout the conflict over the Stamp Act. In Rhode Island, the courts acted at least in part in response to a resolution of the colonial legislature that promised to indemnify all judges and other officials for any damages suffered as a result of their disregard of the act.

New Hampshire was a third colony where the courts remained open. When the superior court adjourned its August 1765 session in October 1765, which was before the effective date of the Stamp Act, it directed that a grand jury and a venire of petit jurors be summoned for its next regular session, in February 1766. When the court reopened in February, however, stamps were required on court documents, and the court clerk refused to accept documents that did not contain them. The judges immediately responded with the following order: "The Justices considering the necessity and expediency for the preservation of the peace and good order of the Province of holding this court and . . . having business done as usual and no stamped paper to be had in this Province, do order and command the clerk of this court to issue all writs, processes and copies as usual, without stamped paper." Passing only implicitly on the constitutionality of the Stamp Act and thus without directly challenging Parliament's power, the justices kept the superior court open and the clerk protected from potential liability for using unstamped paper. Meanwhile New Hampshire's lower courts had continued to function.

The most contentious conflict over the Stamp Act occurred within a divided Court of Common Pleas in Charleston, South Carolina. At the court's first meeting after the effective date of the act, in November 1765, Chief Justice Charles Shinner, a placeman from Ireland for whom the local bar had little respect, sat alone without the presence of any associate judges and "being of opinion that no business can [be] proceeded upon until such stamped paper can be procured," adjourned the November 1765 term.

At the next term, in February 1766, however, matters began to come to a head. Thomas Bee, the attorney for the plaintiff in the case of *Jordan v. Law*, informed the court that he had served a rule to plead on John Rutledge, the defendant's attorney, and that the time for pleading had long expired. Attorney Bee then moved for judgment, "to which Mr. Rutledge said he had no manner of objection. Mr. Manigault of counsel with the plaintiff then spoke very fully in support of the motion as did also Mr. Pinckney, Mr. Parsons and Mr. Rutledge who though not concerned for the plaintiff in this particular case said they were concerned as counsel in a great variety of causes of a similar nature." Only the province's attorney general spoke in opposition to Bee's motion. In view of the "particular circumstances which they [were] now in and the steps" then being taken "to obtain a repeal of the Stamp Act," the court was "unanimously of opinion . . . that no positive determination be given upon the point, but that the same be postponed until the next" term.

At the April 1766 term, Bee again moved for judgment. The nub of Bee's argument was that Magna Carta declared it a wrong "to delay or deny justice to the subject" and that, because of the impossibility of obtaining stamped paper, the Stamp Act had that effect. Accepting this argument, the Court of Common Pleas, by a 4–1 vote, ordered that judgment be entered despite the unavailability of stamped paper. The majority also directed that "the process of this Court be issued out in the usual manner by any person who shall require and apply for the same, that there may no longer be a complaint that justice is either denied or delayed."

Chief Justice Shinner dissented. His view, in essence, was that it was not as a matter of law impossible to obtain stamped paper: the same people who were petitioning the judges to keep the courts open had also conspired with others to make stamped paper unavailable. "No man," he concluded, should "avail himself of his own wrong," and he as a judge could not "deny the legislative power of King, Lords and Commons of Great Britain over the colonies in America." Shinner, in his words, "revere[d] our happy constitution" and was unwilling "to transgress in any instance against a fundamental rule of law."

A month later, when common pleas met again, Justice Lowdnes filed an opinion on behalf of the four-judge majority. The majority had hoped that the chief justice would withdraw his dissent and not "set . . . up the judgment of one judge in opposition to that of the rest of the whole bench, thereby inverting the well known order of judicial determinations, and establishing . . . a precedent that the minority shall conclude the majority." But Shinner did not withdraw his opinion and, indeed, had gone further and directed the officers and ministers of the court to obey his ruling rather than that of the majority. Therefore the majority thought it necessary to file a ten-page opinion recording its reasoning.

The foundation of the majority's reasoning was a finding that, because of the unavailability of stamped paper, compliance with the Stamp Act was impossible. The majority was unwilling to "presume," as had the chief justice, "that the suitors of this Court [were] instrumental in causing the necessity which ha[d] been so prejudicial to themselves." It continued:

> Whatever cause this may be owing to, the effect and consequences are the same; if no business is to be done without stamp paper, and it is absolutely impossible for the Court to procure stamp paper, the inference is, that the Stamp Act in such an exigency would oblige the Courts of Law to be shut up, all business to be remitted and the administration of law and justice to be suspended. Can it be presumed that Parliament meant any such thing or is there one word in the act from the first to the last page of it that gives the least countenance to such an interpretation[?] Could the Parliament intend by this law to abrogate and repeal all precedent acts of Parliament, to unhinge the constitution of the colonies, to unloose the hands of violence and oppression, to introduce anarchy and confusion among us, and to reduce us to a state of outlawry? For to be without law, and to want the means of dispensing the law is one and the same thing. Yet all these consequences unavoidably result from the position that no business can be done at all events, without stamp paper.

In view of "the impossibility . . . of complying with the act," the majority concluded that, at least as construed by the chief justice, the Stamp Act was inapplicable. Because "no power [could] oblige to impossibilities," the court, with an obvious reference to *Bonham's Case*, concluded that the act "enjoin[ed] a thing impossible to be performed" and was therefore "repugnant and against reason and common right, [and] my Lord Coke says is void." Although the opinion did not actually state that the Stamp Act was unconstitutional, it came close to doing so and, at the very least, construed the act to avoid any constitutional difficulties.

Having answered the chief justice, the majority next turned to the court's clerk. From the outset, the clerk, Dougal Campbell, had sided with the chief justice; in April 1766, he had "humbly begged leave to decline paying obedience to the direction[s] of this Court" to enter the judgment in *Jordan v. Law*. "From particular tenderness and indulgence on account of his hitherto dutiful and diligent behavior in office," however, the court did not punish Campbell and merely appointed a replacement, William Mason, as acting clerk.

Apparently Campbell did not permit Mason to act in his stead. In his view, "the Stamp Act did not allow him to pay obedience to the directions of the Court." Accordingly, Campbell refused both to enter judgment in *Jordan v. Law* and to issue writs. He also refused to issue a venire to summon a jury for the May 1766 term. Collectively his acts resulted in "the prevention of justice, and in all probability the total loss of many just demands."

The chief justice spoke on Campbell's behalf and then "quitted the bench." Thereupon the court expressed its shock at the clerk's behavior, which it found "inconsistent with and repugnant to the very idea of that subordination which as a ministerial officer he owe[d] to the Court" and a "total inversion of all law, order, decency, and decorum." It found Campbell guilty of "endeavoring to wrest from the Court, (to whom of right it appertains to construe the laws), their proper jurisdiction" and fined him one hundred pounds. Upon learning from Campbell that the chief justice was still refusing to sign or seal writs, the court also appointed the senior associate justice, Robert Pringel, to act in the chief justice's place.

So far, we have examined four colonies—Massachusetts, Rhode

Island, New Hampshire, and South Carolina—in which courts remained open when the Stamp Act either was held unconstitutional or was otherwise ignored. In two others—Delaware and Maryland—courts also were open. In Delaware, a grand jury refused to return any criminal indictments, which could be prosecuted under the Stamp Act without the use of stamped paper, until the civil courts, where stamps were required, reopened as well; the civil courts accordingly reopened. In Maryland, county courts remained open without requiring stamped paper as early as November 1765, when the Stamp Act first went into effect; the central courts reopened under pressure from the Sons of Liberty at the beginning of April 1766.

In New York some of the judges of the courts of common pleas, apparently in response to a resolution by attorneys to do business without stamped paper, proposed to open the courts in January 1766. They drew up a memorial and presented it to the governor to be recorded in the minutes of the council. The governor, however, refused to entertain it and warned the judges that they would lose their seats on the council as well as on the bench if they opened the courts. Thus, despite the implicit view of judges that the Stamp Act was unconstitutionally null and void and that they should process cases without stamps, the New York courts remained closed.

The highest courts of all the other colonies remained closed as well, but in four other colonies—New Jersey, North Carolina, Pennsylvania, and Virginia—some county courts remained open. In Virginia, at least one lawyer was concerned that closing the local courts might lead people to think that law and order would not be maintained; he also argued that Parliament had no authority to pass the Stamp Act and that the act was therefore null and void and of no effect. Some county courts went even further. When the judges of Accomac County opened court, they warned "that any attorney neglecting to carry on his business in court, under pretence of wanting stamps, should have his suits dismissed." And the judges of neighboring Northampton County responded as follows to an inquiry from its nonjudicial officers whether they would incur any penalties for keeping the court open without using stamped paper: "The said court unanimously declared it to be their opinion that the said act did not bind, affect, or concern the inhabitants of this colony, inasmuch as they conceive the same to be unconstitutional, and that the said officers may proceed in the execution of their respective offices, without incurring any penalty by means thereof."

In short, the marginal argument of James Otis in the *Writs of Assistance Case* in 1761 had become mainstream four years later following Parliament's enactment of the Stamp Act. In Massachusetts, South Carolina, and Virginia, and undoubtedly elsewhere, lawyers were arguing that acts of Parliament against natural equity and the fundamental principles of the constitution were null and void and that courts should invalidate the acts and give them no effect. Moreover, judges in the same three colonies, as well as New York and elsewhere, often on a local, county level, had accepted the argument. [The American doctrine of judicial review thus had emerged out of the long-standing American reality that local people—either county judges, local juries, or the popular, local mobs that steered them—rather than Parliament ultimately determined what constituted American law.]

In the eyes of most twenty-first-century readers, the emergence of judicial review during the Stamp Act controversy appears purely political in nature. Readers today are likely to look upon judicial review simply as one of several weapons used by political opponents of Parliament. Judicial review may have seemed similarly political to many who lived through the Stamp Act crisis. On the other hand, colonials such as James Otis and John Adams may have perceived judicial review differently. They were striving to preserve from Parliamentary change the stable, organic communities in which they and their ancestors had long lived. For them, judicial review was an element of that organic stability. Yet, even from their perspective, something political was occurring. Parliament was attacking the colonial constitution; it was attacking, that is, the political arrangements through which the governments of colonial communities had been constituted. Colonials like Otis and Adams had to decide whether and how to protect their constitution—ultimately a political decision. Thus, in the end, the Stamp Act crisis politicized judicial review, however much its proponents may have tried to ignore that politicization.

Whether a reader today regards as political or purely legal the efforts of James Otis, John Adams, and others who joined them in challenging the constitutionality of the Stamp Act, the fact is that they succeeded. They rendered the Stamp Act if not unconstitutional at least unenforceable and thereby forced Parliament in 1766 to repeal it. But along with the repeal Parliament enacted the Declaratory Act, in which it proclaimed its "full power and authority to make laws and statutes of sufficient force and validity to bind the colonies and people of *America*, subjects of the crown of *Great Britain*, in all cases whatsoever." Next it adopted the Townshend Act, which imposed taxes on colonial trade and commerce.

It was easy to impose taxes, but much more difficult to collect them. Smuggling was a potential issue, and to limit it Charles Townshend, the chancellor of the exchequer who drafted the new tax legislation, proposed a new statutory basis for writs of assistance that would facilitate searches for smuggled goods. In the 1761 *Writs of Assistance Case*, it will be recalled, Oxenbridge Thacher had argued correctly but unsuccessfully that only a court of exchequer had jurisdiction to issue a writ of assistance and that the Massachusetts Superior Court therefore lacked jurisdiction to issue one. Townshend was concerned that this jurisdictional claim could be presented to other colonial courts. He therefore proposed and Parliament enacted legislation specifically granting jurisdiction to the highest court of every colony to issue writs of assistance.

But the Townshend legislation was drafted carelessly. Although it clearly authorized the highest court of every colony to grant writs of assistance, it failed to spell out the nature of those writs. Were they general warrants authorizing a customs official and those assisting him to search as many buildings as he wished at any time during the current monarch's reign without any showing of probable cause? Or was the official required before conducting a search to appear in court, demonstrate probable cause, and then search only the one specific location that the writ of assistance authorized him to search? Townshend clearly intended the former, but the relevant section of the Townshend Act did not explicitly so provide.

American judges, concerned with the fundamental constitutional principle that a man should be "as secure in his House, as a Prince in his Castle," largely construed the act to eliminate constitutional difficulties. It was, as one South Carolina treatise writer declared, "unusual for justices to grant general warrants to search all suspected places." Accordingly, when the colony's attorney general applied in

1769 on behalf of royal customs officials for general writs of assistance, the South Carolina court refused to issue them. Instead, it directed the attorney general "to inform the Custom House Officers . . . that whenever any matter occurred in the execution of their duty that made the aid of the judges necessary they would be ready on proper, special application to give them the fullest assistance."

The Supreme Courts of Pennsylvania and New York reached similar results. When the Crown in 1769 requested the issuance of "a general warrant of assistance" on behalf of "customshouse officers," the Pennsylvania judges, upon "considering the several acts of Parliament relating to this subject, . . . were unanimously of opinion that such a general warrant could not legally be granted, but that the custom house officers should apply for warrants of assistance from time to time as special occasions should call for them." Meanwhile, in New York, the supreme court granted a general writ of assistance in 1768, but refused to do so thereafter. Similarly the chief justice of East Florida declared that he was not "justified by Law to issue General Writs . . . to be lodged in the Hands, & to be executed discretionaly, (perhaps without proper Foundation) at the Will of subordinate Officers, to the injury of the Rights of His Majesty's other loyal Subjects." Other colonies that declined to issue general writs were Connecticut, Georgia, Maryland, Rhode Island, and Virginia, and in Delaware, New Jersey, and North Carolina customs officials did not even bother to apply for writs. Oddly, the only colonies that did not offer difficulty to the Crown were Massachusetts, where the issue of general writs had been resolved in 1761, and New Hampshire, which usually followed Massachusetts law.

These Townshend Act cases were statutory construction cases, not constitutional cases. Unlike the Stamp Act cases, they did not hold an act of Parliament unconstitutional. But they were analogous. Constitutional rights were in the background, and the courts were declining to enforce what judges knew to be the intention of Parliament so as to protect those constitutional rights. Although no American court declared the writs of assistance provision of the Townshend Act void on constitutional grounds, the judiciary's concern with protecting constitutional rights transformed the provision for broad general warrants into something of little effect. The courts thereby put the provision into disuse. Everybody understood what the judges were doing. In the words of England's attorney general, the behavior of the American judges was "a case of obstinate and contumacious refusal to execute an English act of Parliament."

In short, the doctrine of judicial review—the power of courts to refuse to give effect to legislation that trespassed on constitutional rights—was well established in the thirteen American colonies by the 1770s. A series of highly publicized cases had applied the doctrine in one form or another in nearly every one of the colonies. In cases of ambiguous legislation such as the writs of assistance provision of the Townshend Act, courts had interpreted the legislation to avoid constitutional difficulties, had protected constitutional rights, and had thereby given the legislation little effect. In cases of clear legislation such as the Stamp Act, courts had declared the legislation void and thereby upheld the constitution. In less than a decade, James Otis's marginal argument had become a widely accepted practice of American law. As George Mason argued in the 1772 Virginia case of *Robin v. Hardaway*, all human laws "which contradict . . . [the] laws [of God], we are in conscience bound to disobey. Such have been the adjudications of our courts of justice."

CHAPTER FIVE

The State Cases and
the 1787 Convention

The coming of American independence did not halt the development of judicial review that had begun with James Otis's argument in the *Writs of Assistance Case* and matured in the Stamp Act and Townshend Act cases. Lawyers in cases in the 1780s remembered the constitutional arguments that they had made less than twenty years earlier, and judges remembered how earlier courts had ruled on those arguments. Precedent—decisions, indeed, within recent memory—mattered in the post-Revolutionary cases.

Holmes v. Walton, a 1780 New Jersey case, was the first involving judicial review to occur in the aftermath of independence. At issue was a statute authorizing the condemnation of Loyalist property by a six-man rather than a twelve-man jury, as required under the new state constitution. The New Jersey Supreme Court held the statute unconstitutional.

Two years later the Virginia Court of Appeals decided *Commonwealth v. Caton*. After three Loyalists had been convicted of treason, the lower house of the state legislature had pardoned them. At issue was the validity of the pardon. Virginia's treason act provided that pardons were effective only if both houses of the legislature concurred in granting them. The state constitution, however, provided that, in cases that had been prosecuted by the lower house of the legislature, the lower house had power to grant a pardon without the concurrence of the upper house. Recognizing the importance of the case, the court invited other members of the bar, as well as the prosecutor and defense counsel, to present their views. Two important arguments, both in support of judicial review, were made, by Edmund Randolph, the prosecutor and later the first attorney general of the United States, and by St. George Tucker, the professor of law at the College of William and Mary and future editor of the American edition of Blackstone's *Commentaries*.

The grounds on which the judges justified their votes are somewhat unclear, and not all of them decided the case on constitutional grounds. One found the treason act unconstitutional without specifying his reasoning, whereas another stated that he was "against the Power of the Court to declare an Act of the Legislature void." A third refused to state whether, in his view, courts possessed the power of judicial review, and three others said nothing at all about the power. But two of the judges—Edmund Pendleton and George Wythe—addressed judicial review at length, although both upheld the treason act's constitutionality as applied to the facts of the specific case.

Wythe understood it was "his duty to protect a solitary individual against the rapacity of the sovereign" as well as "to protect one branch of the legislature, and, consequently, the whole community, against the usurpations of the other." He accordingly declared that "whenever the proper occasion occurs, I shall feel the duty; and, fearlessly, perform it." Pendleton agreed that all "Powers" had their "limits, the Legislative as well as the others, which if they Pass, it would seem their Act would be void." But he continued: "How far this Court . . . can go in declaring an Act of the Legislature void, because it is repugnant to the Constitution, without exercising the Power of Legislation, from which they are restrained by the same Constitution? is a deep, important, and, I will add, an awful question; from which, however, I will not shrink, if ever it shall become my duty to decide it." He saw no need to address the question in the case before him, however, because he found the treason act and the constitution consistent on the facts of that case. Wythe agreed that the act was constitutional, and four other judges voted as Wythe and Pendleton did. As a result, by a 6–2 vote, the court of appeals held the pardon granted by the lower house alone invalid.

The next case was *Rutgers v. Waddington*, which came before the New York City Mayor's Court in 1784. The case raised a question of the constitutionality of New York State's 1783 trespass act, which gave property owners in New York City who had fled from the city during the British occupation of 1776–1783 a cause of action against those who had used their property in their absence. Waddington, a British merchant, had used Rutgers's brewery from 1778 to 1780 under the authority of the British commissary general and from 1780 to 1783 under the authority of the British military command.

Alexander Hamilton, who represented Waddington, argued that the trespass act was unconstitutional for two reasons. First, he argued that the state's constitution had adopted the common law, that the law of nations was part of the common law, and that under the law of nations an occupying army could license use of property within its power. Second, Hamilton argued that the treaty by which Britain recognized American independence protected from suit those who had acted under British authority during the war and that the treaty constituted law that was paramount to the law of any state.

In his opinion for the court, Mayor James Duane accepted most of Hamilton's argument. He agreed that the law of nations was "a branch of the common law," that "the common law . . . [was] part of the law of the land," and thus that New York was bound by the law of nations. He also agreed that "the foederal compact ha[d] vested Congress with full and exclusive power to make peace and war," that the treaty of peace with Britain "implie[d] an amnesty and oblivion of damages and injuries in the war," and "that no state in th[e] union [could] alter or abridge, in a single point, the foederal articles or the treaty." Still, he refused to hold the trespass act unconstitutional. Duane stated that, if the legislature "think[s] fit *positively* to enact a law, there is no power which can controul them. When the main object of such a law is clearly expressed, and the intention manifest, the Judges are not at liberty, altho' it appears to them to be *unreasonable*, to reject it; for this were to set the *judicial* above the legislative, which would be subversive of all government." But, because Duane found the trespass act not clearly expressed, he was prepared to construe it to be consistent with constitutional values. He concluded that "the repeal of the law of nations, or any interference with it, could not have been in contemplation, in our opinion, when the Legislature passed this statute, and we think ourselves bound to exempt that law from its operation." Accordingly, he held, consistent with his understanding of the law of nations, that Waddington had not trespassed on Rutgers's land and did not need to pay rent to Rutgers for the period between 1780 and 1783, when he had occupied the land under British military authority. In so holding, Duane effectively struck down the trespass act in the guise of interpretation.

The three cases just discussed all raised politically controversial questions about the treatment of Loyalists. The fourth case in the post-Revolutionary era involving the issue of judicial review, however, was uncontroversial. In the 1785 *Symsbury Case* the Connecticut Superior Court invalidated an act of its colonial legislature. In 1670, Connecticut had granted land to predecessors of the proprietors of the town of Symsbury; sixteen years later, Connecticut granted some of the same land to the proprietors of Hartford and Windsor. Four decades after this second grant, the legislature authorized a survey of the boundaries of Symsbury—a survey that found the twice-granted land within the boundaries of Hartford or Windsor, not Symsbury. The legislature by statute then confirmed the surveyors' findings. The Connecticut Superior Court found, however, that the land in dispute had originally been granted to Symsbury and that the subsequent legislative act confirming the surveyors' findings "could not legally operate to curtail the land before granted to the proprietors of Symsbury, without their consent." The act was therefore void.

Two other controversial cases were decided in 1787. *Trevett v. Weeden* arose in Rhode Island in regard to a statute requiring creditors to accept the state's paper money as legal tender, establishing a penalty for refusals to accept the money, and authorizing suits to recover the penalty without trial by jury. At bottom, *Trevett v. Weeden* was about Rhode Island's highly controversial, pro-debtor, paper-money policies, although Weeden's counsel argued mainly on the ground that the statute violated his client's constitutional right to a trial by jury. The Rhode Island court implicitly challenged its state's policies when it gave judgment in Weeden's favor, with three of the five judges on the court stating that their judgment rested on constitutional grounds.

Bayard v. Singleton, which arose in North Carolina, returned to the controversial issue of Loyalists. *Bayard* was a suit by a plaintiff who claimed title to land from a Loyalist whose property had been seized by the state. Pursuant to a statute that directed courts to dismiss title suits whenever a defendant submitted an affidavit showing that his title was derived from the state following a seizure from a Loyalist, the defendant moved to dismiss. In response, the plaintiff, relying on a constitutional provision that "in all controversies at law respecting property, the ancient mode of trial by jury . . . shall remain sacred and inviolable," challenged the constitutionality of the statute. The court agreed: "The constitution (which the judicial power was bound to take notice of as much as of any other law whatever,) standing in full force as the fundamental law of the land, notwithstanding the act on which the present motion was grounded, the same act must of course, in that instance, stand as abrogated and without any effect." The court accordingly directed that the case be tried by a jury, which subsequently returned a verdict for the defendant.

In addition to these six cases, at least two and perhaps several other New Hampshire cases held unconstitutional a statute depriving plaintiffs in suits under ten pounds value of the right to trial by jury. Thus, by the time of the meeting of the federal Constitutional Convention in 1787, at least eight cases in seven states—Connecticut, New Hampshire, New Jersey, New York, North Carolina, Rhode Island, and Virginia—either had held legislation unconstitutional or had construed legislation to avoid constitutional difficulties. In most respects, these eight cases between 1780 and 1787 simply continued practices that had emerged during the Stamp Act and Townshend Act controversies of the 1760s.

In one respect, however, the cases from the 1780s were profoundly different. In the 1760s cases, judicial review was being deployed against a foreign legislature—Parliament—to protect interests of the inhabitants of a colonial polity over which a court had jurisdiction. As shown in chapter 1, American courts and juries in the first six decades of the eighteenth century had frequently upheld the law of communities from which they were drawn against law imposed from outside; the 1760s cases did nothing different. The results of the 1760s cases were consistent with the constitutional will of the people, and therefore there was little opposition to the exercise of judicial review; what little opposition occurred came mainly from officeholders appointed by and beholden to the Crown.

In the 1780s cases, in contrast, the legislation that was invalidated had been enacted by representatives of localities. Those representatives were understood to reflect the views of their constituents and, in some states, were formally bound by those views. As a result, most people viewed legislatures as sovereign lawmaking bodies. In striking down legislation, courts thus were overriding the duly enacted policies of their own communities, not the policies of some distant Parliament. In the *Symsbury Case* and the New Hampshire cases, the courts were upholding the right to trial by jury, which was not a judgment that led to significant political opposition. But in the five remaining cases, the courts, unlike the courts of the 1760s, were not supporting local people against an outside legislature. On the contrary, the doctrine of judicial review was being deployed in favor of outsiders or disfavored groups within the community by overturning what the sovereign legislature of the community had enacted.

Four of the cases—*Holmes v. Walton*, *Commonwealth v. Caton*, *Rutgers v. Waddington*, and *Bayard v. Singleton*—reflected efforts to protect an exceedingly unpopular group: Loyalists, who had opposed American independence. *Commonwealth v. Caton* sought unsuccessfully to reprieve from death three men convicted of treason after those men had failed to obtain pardons from all branches of the Virginia government legislatively required to join in granting pardons. The three other cases involved judicial recognition of Loyalist property rights in contexts in which legislatures had sought to deprive the Loyalists of those rights. *Trevett v. Weeden* was a case in which Rhode Island's highest court struck down legislation making that state's paper money legal tender, thereby favoring the interests of creditors, another unpopular group, against the interests of a popular group, debtors, that the legislature had favored.

It is not surprising that strong opposition arose to several of these judicial exercises. In Rhode Island, for example, the legislature summoned the five judges who had decided *Trevett v. Weeden* and forced four of them off the bench. In New York, the lower house of the legislature criticized the *Rutgers* decision and warned that if one court could "dispense with, an act in direct violation of a plain and known law of the state, all other Courts either superior or inferior may do the like." The judicial review cases of the 1780s were political in senses in which the 1760s cases had not been. Of course, both the Stamp Act and the Townshend Act had had political salience that had led to profound political consequences. But the courts in a significant way did not take sides in the political dispute; American courts in holding acts of Parliament unconstitutional simply gave effect to the united will—the consensus—of their communities. In the 1780s, in contrast, the courts took sides in political conflicts over which their communities were divided.

When the framers of the federal Constitution came together in Philadelphia in 1787 and then presented their product to the states for ratification, judicial review thus was politically contentious. It could lead to political upheaval. As James Monroe noted at the time, judicial review was a subject "calculated to create heats and animosities." John Dickinson, for one, accordingly "thought no such power ought to exist," and John Mercer, another delegate in Philadelphia, "disapproved of the Doctrine that the Judges as expositors of the Constitution should have authority to declare a law void." The most important early opponent of judicial review, perhaps, was James Madison, who wrote that its practice would make "the Judiciary Department paramount in fact to the Legislature, which was never intended and can never be proper."

Madison's opposition to judicial review was consistent with his proposal of a congressional negative on state legislation—his plan that the states submit all of their legislation to Congress, which would determine its consistency with federal law and the federal Constitution and invalidate legislation that was inconsistent. But the convention rejected Madison's plan and turned instead to the supremacy clause, as enforced by the federal judiciary, as the mechanism for ensuring the consistency of state law with federal law. That decision not only gave the federal courts jurisdiction to hold state laws unconstitutional; it also meant that the judiciary would need power to declare acts of Congress unconstitutional.

An example will illustrate why judicial review of the constitutionality of federal legislation is implicit in a grant of jurisdiction to review state legislation. Consider, for example, Rhode Island's laws making its paper money legal tender for payment of debts. Those laws were, in fact, invalidated under the federal Constitution's contract clause. But assume that they had not been so invalidated and that Congress, pursuant to its power to regulate commerce, had responded by requiring the payment of all debts in notes issued by the Bank of the United States. Many questioned whether Congress had power to charter a bank and undoubtedly would have questioned the constitutionality of the congressional statute just proposed. Wouldn't the Supreme Court have had to pass on the constitutionality of such an act of Congress before it could have considered whether Rhode Island's laws were invalid because inconsistent with that act? A federal government of unlimited power is, after all, inconsistent with the basic design of the constitutional system, which created a federal government of limited power with the federal judiciary as the policeman of the limits.

A second example might be helpful. Assume that the constitution of some particular state currently gives defendants in felony prosecutions a right to trial by jury. But Congress, with a goal of increasing the rate of conviction in felony cases, enacts a statute prohibiting jury trials in criminal cases in that state. Of course, federal law trumps state law. But what constitutes federal law? The congressional statute? Or the federal Constitution, which may not permit Congress to enact a law applying only to one state and which also may guarantee a right to jury trial? Isn't it always necessary for a court, before holding that federal law overrides state law, to determine what federal law is? And, when a federal statute is alleged to be in conflict with the federal Constitution, doesn't the court have to give effect to the Constitution rather than the statute if a conflict does exist?

In short, once the framers decided to turn to the courts to ensure the supremacy of federal law over state law, they inevitably delegated to those courts jurisdiction to determine the meaning of federal law. And in determining the meaning of federal law in the event of a conflict between an act of Congress and the Constitution, courts had to have power to give effect to the Constitution and to invalidate the congressional act. If courts could not invalidate or place an otherwise limiting construction on a congressional act that purported to override state law, states could never win and would necessarily lose whenever they challenged such acts.

Thus, men like Elbridge Gerry argued that judges "by their exposition of the laws" would have "a power of deciding on their constitutionality." George Mason agreed that courts "could declare an unconstitutional law void," and even James Madison came to support judicial review. At the convention, for example, Madison argued for judicial review in "cases of a Judiciary Nature" and later, in debates on the Bill of Rights, he maintained that "independent tribunals of justice [would] consider themselves in a peculiar manner the guardians of those rights." And the most famous defense of judicial review came from Alexander Hamilton in *Federalist No. 78*.

In the aftermath of the convention and ratification debate, during the decade of the 1790s, the number of state cases in which the issue of judicial review arose accordingly multiplied. Because of imprecision in court records and because judges in some cases refused to apply statutes but failed to explain their reasoning, it is impossible to identify a precise number of judicial review cases. All that can be said with certainty is that, between the time of the Constitutional Convention in 1787 and the decision of *Marbury v. Madison* in 1803, more than thirty cases involving judicial review arose.

Roughly half of those cases invalidated statutes by which legislatures had removed private disputes from the judicial process and granted judgment—a practice that had been common prior to the American Revolution and continued thereafter. But the practice violated post-Revolutionary concepts of separation of powers, and many courts, like the Connecticut court in the *Symsbury Case*, accordingly struck the statutes down. Another quarter of the cases, like the New Hampshire cases of the 1780s, deprived litigants of the right to a trial by jury. These two categories of cases, which had aroused little opposition and received little public notice in the 1780s, together amounted to approximately three-fourths of all the judicial review cases between 1787 and 1803. As in the earlier decade, they aroused little opposition and received little public notice.

There were cases in the 1790s, however, of the sort that had divided American communities in the 1780s. Thus, two 1791 Rhode Island cases held that the state's legal tender act was "superseded" or "*virtually repealed*" by the adoption of the federal Constitution. Similarly a federal circuit court struck down a Rhode Island statute that had granted particular debtors a three-year moratorium against suits to collect their debts, and a federal court in North Carolina struck down a statute confiscating Loyalists' contract claims. Another 1801 Kentucky case suggested that a state statute limiting damages to 15 percent of what the parties had agreed in their contract might be invalid under the federal Constitution's contract clause, although the court actually invalidated the statute on other grounds. Most significant of all was *Ware v. Hylton*, in which the Supreme Court in 1796 held unconstitutional a Virginia statute canceling claims of British creditors against debtors who had paid the amount due on their debts to the Virginia treasury.

No opposition materialized in response to these decisions. Indeed, when the federal court in Rhode Island struck down the three-year moratorium that the state legislature had granted to particular debtors, the legislature responded that "in conformity to [the] decision of the Circuit Court, [it] would not grant to any individual an exemption from arrests and attachments, for his private debts." Of course, all these decisions were consistent with the determination of the 1787 Constitutional Convention authorizing the judiciary to supervise the consistency of state law with federal law. The decisions also may have reflected an understanding that two major political issues— the one concerning debtor-creditor relations and the other, Loyalist claims—had been resolved during the course of the political debate culminating in the ratification of the federal Constitution. In short, courts in the 1790s were resolving without difficulty what earlier had been divisive questions but had become judicial matters on which the political community had largely come to agree.

Courts were also passing on the constitutionality of statutes that would raise divisive issues at later times in American history, but were unproblematic in the 1790s. These included a statute prohibiting the building of wooden structures in certain parts of Philadelphia; a statute prohibiting state officeholders from holding federal offices as well; a statute prohibiting participation in the African slave trade; a statute confirming titles of Connecticut settlers in Luzerne County, Pennsylvania; a Vermont statute expropriating land given to the Anglican church; a statute giving lower federal courts concurrent jurisdiction with the Supreme Court over suits against foreign consuls; statutes providing for takings of land without payment of just compensation; and statutes imposing duties on judges in addition to those of the court to which they had been appointed. Another case prohibited retroactive application of a statute to a person who had no notice of it when committing the prohibited act, and yet another addressed the issue of the power of state courts to naturalize prospective citizens. Some of these cases received public attention from printed media, but none of them generated lasting political conflict among competing interest groups.

In addition, the Supreme Court in the 1790s twice confronted the issue of judicial review. In *Hylton v. United States*, a taxpayer argued that a tax on carriages was a direct tax and hence was unconstitutional because not properly apportioned among the states. The Court, however, upheld the tax by ruling it was not a direct one. In the aftermath of adoption of the Eleventh Amendment, the Court also dismissed three pending cases in which individuals were suing state governments. In *Chisholm v. Georgia* the Court had previously upheld the right of individuals to bring such suits under the 1789 Judiciary Act, but like Rhode Island courts in the aftermath of ratification of the federal Constitution, the Supreme Court understood that ratification of the Eleventh Amendment rendered its reading of the Judiciary Act unconstitutional. Hence it dismissed the three cases. Although the doctrine of judicial review was never discussed, the dismissal of the three cases can be understood only as a holding that the reading of the Judiciary Act that had allowed the three plaintiffs to file suit had become unconstitutional as a result of the Eleventh Amendment's adoption.

In conclusion, by the time *Marbury v. Madison* came before the Supreme Court in 1803, judicial review was firmly implanted in American law. The practice of American courts, at times through judges and at other times through juries, of declining to apply legislation they found unjust had been in place for a century. The specific doctrine that courts should refuse to apply legislation they found unconstitutional had been elaborated by James Otis forty years earlier. Although the doctrine had been rejected at the time by the Massachusetts Superior Court, Otis propagated it in his widely distributed pamphlet, *The Rights of the British Colonies Asserted and Proved*. Within a year, courts in half of the American colonies had adopted the doctrine, and by the end of the 1760s Otis's argument had been accepted by a majority of American courts in writs of assistance cases analogous to Otis's 1761 case.

Over the next thirty years lawyers continued to argue that courts should hold specific legislative acts unconstitutional; sometimes courts rejected the argument, but at other times they accepted it and either held legislation void or interpreted it to render it consistent with constitutional principle. When the draftsmen of the federal Constitution turned to the judiciary to supervise the consistency of state law with federal law, they implicitly empowered the judiciary to supervise as well the consistency of Congress's legislation with the Constitution. Lawyers opposed to Congress's carriage tax accordingly argued in the *Hylton* case that the tax was unconstitutional. The Supreme Court rejected their argument, but several years later, when adoption of the Eleventh Amendment outlawed suits against states, the Court *sub silentio* held that the amendment trumped its prior reading of the 1789 Judiciary Act allowing such suits. As Alexander Hamilton had explained, the logic that when an irreconcilable conflict existed between a statute and the constitution, the latter fundamental law had to prevail was impeccable.

CHAPTER SIX

The Politics of Constitutional Change

We saw in chapter 2 how the routine, day-by-day practices of governance in mid-eighteenth-century America depended to some significant degree on the existence of an established Anglo-American constitutional structure that colonials could neither alter nor control. In this chapter, we shall examine how, after the end in 1763 of the Seven Years' War, known in America as the French and Indian War, that structure became unhinged.

The war transformed the imperial structure in two profound respects. For the first six decades of the eighteenth century, French control of Canada, the Great Lakes, and the entire Mississippi basin had placed the western boundary of the British North American colonies at the crest of the Appalachian range, which runs through northern New England, central New York and Pennsylvania, and western Virginia and North Carolina. The French and their Indian allies had inhibited land-hungry American colonials from establishing agricultural settlements on the western side of the Appalachians. But when a British army captured Quebec in 1760 and occupied Montreal the next year, French power was doomed. By the 1763 treaty ending the war, France transferred the city of New Orleans and all of the Mississippi basin west of the Mississippi River to Spain. France ceded the remainder of its territory on the North American continent to Great Britain.

With the elimination of French power from North America, land speculators and prospective settlers could hope that settlement of the trans-Appalachian west would be encouraged. Their hopes were set back, however, when the ministry in London issued the Proclamation of 1763, which limited settlement to lands east of the crest of the Appalachians. But the possibility of trans-Appalachian settlement did not go away. French and Indian opposition to settlement could remove its possibility from the political and social agenda of British North Americans, but London's opposition could not. Americans regarded the Proclamation of 1763 as a grievance throughout the remainder of the colonial era, and by ignoring the proclamation and establishing homes and farms west of the proclamation line, a few of them even challenged London's capacity to enforce it.

The second significant impact of the Seven Years' War was on the British government's budget. Great Britain had incurred enormous financial costs during the war, which had created a burgeoning national debt. The war also had left Great Britain with rising expenditures resulting from increased military obligations in newly acquired territories such as Canada. The end result was increasing debt service and rising taxes. When the ministry in London looked for new sources of revenue to cover its growing fiscal needs, it came to the judgment that its North American colonies, which were among the principal beneficiaries of the war, ought to be taxed to pay for its costs. Parliament agreed and enthusiastically passed the Sugar Act of 1764 and then the Stamp Act of 1765.

America was never again the same. Colonial leaders organized widespread resistance to parliamentary taxation, and they succeeded in procuring the repeal of both the Sugar Act and the Stamp Act. But Parliament insisted upon its power to tax in the Declaratory Act of 1766, which proclaimed Parliament's sovereign power to legislate for its North American colonies in all cases whatsoever, and in subsequent years it periodically imposed limited taxes. Meanwhile, the colonials, who had learned how to mount continent-wide resistance during the Stamp Act crisis, maintained their opposition to Parliament's sovereignty claim.

This is not the place to analyze the vast historical literature on the pre-Revolutionary constitutional conflict nor to discuss, in any detail, the conflict itself. It will suffice to note that violent rebellion broke out in April 1775 at Lexington and Concord. A year later, on July 4, 1776, the Declaration of Independence was adopted, and the thirteen colonies of British North America became the independent United States.

At the outset of the War of Independence, most rebelling colonists aimed not so much to change as to preserve the basic structure of the political system under which they had lived prior to what they viewed as Parliament's attempts between 1763 and 1775 to subvert it. In particular, most Americans wished to preserve a political order that generally required officials to govern according to established, largely unchanging values or principles that nearly all citizens accepted as right or otherwise legitimate.

Nevertheless, independence significantly reshaped American politics by introducing a new political style in stark contrast to the mid-eighteenth-century style of government by appealing to an established consensus. Over the course of the next several years, the Continental Congress had to raise and support an army, appoint commanding generals, negotiate with foreign powers, and strive to place national power on a firm constitutional footing. Connected with this final task was the governance of the vast territories in the trans-Appalachian West that the United States would acquire from Great Britain in the 1783 peace treaty acknowledging American independence. In performing these tasks, Congress and other national officials had to make choices among possible policies that were in conflict with each other—choices that favored some American interests over others and thus could not be made on the basis of principles or values with which nearly everyone agreed.

These national issues impacted local politics. Most significant of all were the divisions in local communities resulting from the Revolutionary struggle itself, as citizens who identified themselves as Patriots came into conflict with Loyalists, those who remained committed to the cause of Parliament and the Crown. These conflicts sundered communities and often resulted in the exile of Loyalists and the confiscation of their properties.

With the ratification of the Articles of Confederation, a new Confederation Congress came into being in 1781. But national political issues did not go away, nor did they cease to have an impact on local communities. Several issues growing out of the War of Independence and the 1783 peace accord were of special importance.

In order to obtain peace and independence and to secure British evacuation of all outposts in the newly recognized American territories, Congress had agreed in the 1783 treaty that individual British creditors would suffer no impediments to the collection of debts owed to them by Americans. But several states refused to honor this provision in the treaty and placed various impediments in the path of

British creditors. Prospective lenders in Great Britain, knowing they would face future impediments as creditors, responded by tightening credit, while the British government reacted by refusing to evacuate outposts in the western portions of the new United States that the 1783 treaty had obligated it to surrender. As a result, Americans seeking to borrow money found it more difficult and expensive to do so, and those seeking to settle or otherwise exploit the West found the British army and its Indian allies in their path.

These actions by several American states, by British lenders, and by the British government created political divisions in local American communities that would endure into the early nineteenth century. On the one side were established farmers who had borrowed money in the past and now found repayment difficult or undesirable; they did not want Congress to interfere with state policies that made debt collection more difficult and created a possibility that they might avoid full repayment of their debts. Pitted against them were pioneers who found the British blocking their westward movement and business entrepreneurs seeking to borrow funds to expand their operations; they wanted a stronger national Congress that could compel the states to obey the peace treaty and otherwise advance their interests in westward expansion or international commerce. Clashes between these groups reverberated on the local, state, and national levels.

Above all, independence destroyed the constitutional order that had existed for a century in the British North American world. No longer were fundamental questions such as the distribution of power among various levels of government, the continuance of religious establishments, and the freedom of American merchants to trade abroad resolved by an imperial law that the colonies had little direct power to control. Independence compelled Americans to resolve such questions anew, often on a national rather than a local basis. Independence meant that newly independent Americans, unlike their colonial ancestors, would routinely need to make choices among competing policies and, as a result of those choices, structure the world in which they wanted to live. The post-Revolutionary generation's grappling with these questions portended social discord in both state and national politics and during the last two decades of the eighteenth century provoked some of the most vituperative conflict that has ever occurred in American political history.

The revolutionary struggle and the attainment of independence also transformed American society and politics ideologically. In discarding British rule and reconstituting their governments, Americans proclaimed that all law springs from popular will as codified in legislation. If the people could remake their government, it followed, the *Maryland Journal* declared in 1787, that the lawmaking power of the people must be "original, inherent, and unlimited by human authority." A preacher who spoke to the Massachusetts legislature in 1782 identified popular will as "the only rational source of power," while in the next year the *Connecticut Courant* wrote that there was "an original, underived and incommunicable authority and supremacy in the collective body of the people to whom all delegated power must submit and from whom there is no appeal."

This concept of legislation as the creation of new law by the people or their representatives proved practically significant after independence because groups such as religious dissenters and westward expansionists used it to promote their interests. Before the Revolution, policies imposed by London had tended to restrict westward expansion and to require that dissenters support established churches. Once independent Americans could formulate their own policies, however, both religious dissenters and westward expansionists campaigned to revise established policies. Legislatures frequently responded by changing inherited rules and practices, and in the process changed themselves as well. By enacting new law, legislatures reinforced the ideology of popular lawmaking power and forged an active, creative legislative process in lieu of one that had depended on the derivation of rules from preexisting shared principles.

This transformation occurred, however, in a society unprepared to blithely abandon the pre-Revolutionary ideal that human law was unchanging and that it needed to conform to fundamental principles of divine or natural law. The older ideal persisted throughout the late 1770s and the 1780s.

Post-Revolutionary Americans continued to maintain, in the words of one Fourth of July speaker in Savannah, Georgia, in 1788, that they could rationally "define the rights of nature" and learn "how to search into, to distinguish, and to comprehend, the principles of physical, moral, religious, and civil liberty." Believing, like Alexander Hamilton, an eminent attorney in the 1780s and later secretary of the treasury, in "eternal principles of social justice," Americans, such as the residents of Salem, New Jersey, in the mid-1780s, objected to legislation that was "founded not upon the principles of Justice, but upon the Right of the Sword" and for which "no other Reason [could] be given . . . than because the Legislature had the Power and Will to enact such a Law." According to a 1786 article in the *Providence Gazette*, legislators who enacted laws that "violate[d] . . . fundamental principles . . . [were] substituting *power* for *right*." Similarly, James Madison, arguing at the time of the Constitutional Convention for a congressional power to negate state legislation, noted in a letter to George Washington, the Revolutionary commander-in-chief who would soon become president, that America needed "some disinterested & dispassionate umpire" to control "disputes between different passions & interests in the State[s]."

In short, many Americans even after the Revolution continued to believe that government should articulate and apply fundamental principles dispassionately, neutrally, and objectively, rather than yield to a mere electoral majority. Some, like Madison, thought that legislatures, not courts, should guard fundamental legal principles, while others, like Hamilton, argued that courts as well as legislatures should do so. But since courts throughout the 1780s were still generally considered an undifferentiated segment of the executive branch, the important issue for that decade was not whether the legislative, executive, or judicial branch should ensure the conformity of law to fundamental standards of right, but whether any institution should.

At times during that decade, legislatures received criticism for failing to protect those fundamental standards. Arguments were made, for instance, at the Virginia convention that ratified the federal Constitution against a Virginia act that had condemned to death an alleged highway robber "without any proof better than vague reports . . . [,] without being confronted with his accusers and witnesses, [and] without the privilege of calling for evidence in his behalf." To those who believed that law must adhere to immutable principles that transcend popular will, "this arbitrary deprivation of life, the dearest gift of God to man," was neither "consistent with the genius of republican government" nor "compatible with the spirit of freedom"; they could "not contemplate it without horror" and hoped that the new

Constitution would render legislation contrary to established fundamental principles invalid.

But others took a different view. One leading intellectual, Noah Webster, argued in 1787 that the collective body of the people possessed "plenary power" to make law and that if the people were to be granted an "unlimited power to do *right*," then they must also be granted "an unlimited power to do *wrong*." Authorizing any group to nullify acts of the people, according to a North Carolina delegate at the 1787 federal Constitutional Convention, "would be more despotic than the Roman Decemvirate," for who could then "check or control" the nullifiers.

As we saw in chapter 5, state courts during the 1780s also heard demands for the protection of fundamental rights. Sometimes, as in the New York case of *Rutgers v. Waddington*, the "supremacy of the Legislature . . . *positively* to enact a law" was pitted explicitly against "the rights of human nature" and the "law of nature." As late as the early 1790s, however, the line between believers in popular sovereignty and believers in supreme fixed principles was rarely so plainly drawn. One could still believe simultaneously in the people's power to make law and in the immutability of the principles underlying law. Although it appreciated and accepted popular lawmaking, the Revolutionary generation did not abandon older notions that law made by the people must not violate rights that Americans had proclaimed immutably theirs in the struggle with England. New and old ideas coexisted as the Revolutionary generation, believing in the people's inherent goodness, simply assumed that all laws made by the people would be consistent with fundamental rights.

As the 1790s progressed, however, this ambivalent legal ideology proved merely transitory and diverged into two clearer, more coherent points of view. One sought to resolve all issues according to the will of the people, while the other sought to resolve them according to fixed principles of law. The appearance of these competing ideologies was closely related to the division in American politics in the 1790s between Federalists, who generally viewed law as a reflection of fixed and transcendent principles, and Republicans, who considered it the embodiment of popular will.

Future Federalists and Republicans first divided over the seemingly trivial issue of the chief executive's title—a matter that raised specters of monarchism. Even more divisive was the economic program of Secretary of the Treasury Alexander Hamilton. His plans to fund the national debt, which would require higher taxes, and to create a national bank, which portended tighter credit, stirred a more significant controversy. However, historians generally agree that the first truly national political organizations arose in the mid-1790s in response to the French Revolution and to the signing of Jay's Treaty with Great Britain. These two events forced Americans to choose sides in the worldwide struggle between Britain and France that began in 1793, and for many the choice posed difficult ideological issues. Some Americans found themselves horrified by the excesses of the French Revolution during the early 1790s and by its culmination in the politically driven executions of the Reign of Terror; others, while not approving of the death and violence, remained convinced that the French republican movement would ultimately warrant American sympathy. Similarly, some thought that John Jay paid too high a price for British withdrawal from the Northwest Territory when he agreed in his treaty to have the federal government, in return, pay Revolutionary era debts still owed to British creditors.

The political divisions of the mid-1790s reflected ideological concerns as well. For example, the Federalists saw in Jefferson and the Republicans many of the threats to religion, to life, and to property that they found so horrifying in French revolutionaries. The election of 1800, according to one Federalist campaign tract, would require voters to select either "GOD—AND A RELIGIOUS PRESIDENT; or impiously declare for JEFFERSON—AND NO GOD!!!"

This widespread Federalist concern over Jefferson's lack of traditional religious belief gained credence from the efforts of prominent elements in the Jeffersonian coalition in states such as Massachusetts and Virginia to pull down the state-supported churches that those colonies had erected at the time of their earliest settlements. For people who lived in an age that had had little experience with societies that had maintained their stability without the assistance of such established churches, it was plausible to fear, as did a Federalist preacher in one 1800 election sermon, that if "the restraints of religion [were] once broken down, as they infallibly would be, by leaving the subject of public worship to the humors of the multitude,

. . . we might well defy all human wisdom and power to support and preserve order and government in the State[s]."

If the Federalists were convinced that conferral of power upon Republicans would subvert morality and lead to violence and anarchy, the Republicans were equally convinced that if allowed to retain power, the Federalists would subvert republican liberties and rule autocratically. These fears of a Federalist conspiracy to pervert American liberties came to a climax during the administration of President John Adams, who held office from 1797 to 1801. It was during his term that Congress for the first time in American history imposed a direct tax, voted to establish a standing army and navy, and adopted the Alien and Sedition Acts, pursuant to which Jeffersonian editors were sent to jail for criticizing government policies.

In short, clear-cut party divisions had emerged by the second half of the 1790s. On one side stood the Republicans, avowing in the words of James Madison "the doctrine that mankind are capable of governing themselves," and accused by their opponents of scheming "to introduce a new order of things as it respects *morals* and *politics*, *social* and *civil* duties." Opposite them stood the Federalists, claiming in the words of the *New England Palladium* to preserve "that virtue [which] is the only permanent basis of a Republic," and accused of attempting to restore monarchical government.

Both parties were internally divided, of course, and not everyone adhered rigidly to his party's ideology. Some statesmen continued to believe that popular will did not inevitably conflict with fundamental standards of right and that law and governmental policy could accordingly reflect both. Nonetheless, when forced to choose, those who styled themselves Federalists generally proclaimed their preference for customary standards, while those who saw themselves as Republicans generally proclaimed their allegiance to the people's will.

These two competing political theories were deeply rooted in still fresh American political experiences; they responded to ardently felt political needs. Republicans in 1800 could look back upon a quarter-century of fervid political activity during which a majority of the people had transformed the American constitutional landscape. In light of this, Republicans could plausibly hold that the popular majority would secure revolutionary improvements in government through continued exertion.

Federalists, on the other hand, looked back to a different governmental tradition. They focused upon the workings of local government, which, even after twenty-five years of revolutionary transformation, continued to function without falling under the arbitrary control of those in positions of power. Federalists recognized a tradition, that is, of government by customary norms whose validity all right-thinking people accepted. That such traditional government seemed under attack in 1800 and unable to resolve every political issue was not startling; eighteenth century government-by-consensus had always been somewhat unstable and unequipped to resolve all problems. Nevertheless, it had succeeded in many matters, and even its partial success offered hope to those in 1800 who dreaded government solely by majority will.

Marbury v. Madison came before the Supreme Court immediately after the conflict between these two approaches to politics had come to a head in the election of 1800, in which Thomas Jefferson defeated John Adams's reelection bid, and after John Marshall, *Marbury*'s author, had been appointed in 1801 by the lame-duck Adams as chief justice of the United States. Before turning to *Marbury* itself, however, we need to examine the background of its author.

CHAPTER SEVEN

John Marshall

John Marshall, who eventually would author *Marbury v. Madison*, was born in 1755 in the then frontier settlement of Germantown, in Prince William County, Virginia. He was the eldest of fifteen children of Mary Randolph Keith, who shared a common ancestry with leading Virginia families such as the Jeffersons, the Randolphs, and the Lees, and of Thomas Marshall, who was the American agent for Lord Fairfax, the British nobleman who owned immense tracts of land in northern Virginia. As a prominent member of his community, Thomas Marshall was active in its governance and served nearly continuously from 1759 until the American Revolution as a justice of the peace and at various times as county surveyor, sheriff, and parish vestryman. After 1769, he also represented his county, Fauquier, which had split off from Prince William, in the House of Burgesses.

As a youth, John Marshall thus was in a good position from which to observe the workings of Virginia's government. Upon attaining the age of twenty in 1775, he became a participant of sorts when he joined a militia unit in which his father held a position of command and marched off to Great Bridge, where he participated in a battle that drove the British army from Virginia soil. Seven months later, he accepted a commission as a lieutenant in the Continental army and spent the next four years at the side of his father's old friend, George Washington, among other places, at Valley Forge.

Marshall's military service was important to his subsequent career for three reasons. First, it turned him into a committed nationalist. As he worked with men from various parts of the new United States, he lost whatever parochialism he may have had and grew in appreciating the common interests of all Americans. Moreover, as he watched his fellow soldiers suffer from lack of food and other supplies, especially at Valley Forge, he recognized the importance of a strong national government having the capacity to furnish the military's needs.

Second, Marshall's service in the Continental army made him a protégé of George Washington. Washington promptly recognized Marshall's extraordinary talent, added him to his headquarters staff, and worked closely with him thereafter. Marshall, in turn, revered Washington as the great leader of the American cause, accepted political direction from Washington as long as the general lived, and ultimately became Washington's first biographer.

Third, the time that John Marshall spent in the army honed his skills as a leader and as a shaper of consensus. During his years of service, Marshall acted as a builder of morale and of dedication to the cause of American independence. He played that role, moreover, at a time when Continental officers had little coercive power over their troops and had to lead by example and by demonstrating fairness. Later, as chief justice of the United States, he would be in a comparable position. He would have little coercive power either over his fellow justices or over the nation as a whole, and he would have to build support for his judgments by convincing others that they were fair and sound and that they were derived from his allegiance to American liberty and constitutionalism.

Late in 1779, John Marshall was discharged from the army and went home to Virginia. Marshall quickly set his sights on becoming a lawyer and registered at the College of William and Mary for the law course taught by George Wythe, who had been Thomas Jefferson's law tutor and had been named to the first professorship of law in an American college during Jefferson's governorship of Virginia. Prior to attending Wythe's law lectures, Marshall had had little formal education: for one year, he had attended a school about one hundred miles from his home that was taught by a local clergyman, and then he had been tutored at home for an additional year by a recent college graduate from Britain. Nonetheless, by the end of the two years, Marshall was transcribing the poetry of Pope and reading Horace and Livy in Latin. Marshall also claimed that, prior to his entering military service at the age of twenty, he had been reading William Blackstone's four-volume *Commentaries on the Laws of England*.

Marshall studied at William and Mary during the spring and early summer of 1780. He compiled the usual set of notes for a law student, consisting of an alphabetical arrangement of information on various legal subjects that a practitioner would need when preparing for court appearances, and then set off in midsummer of 1780 to begin his practice in the new state capital of Richmond. There can be little doubt that John Marshall proved to be a lawyer of exceptional ability, and within the space of a few years, he had become one of the leading advocates—perhaps the leading advocate—in all of Virginia. Indeed, Marshall was so well respected that when Edmund Randolph was elected state governor in 1786, he urged his clients to turn to the young John Marshall, then only thirty-one years old, to be their attorney.

Meanwhile, Marshall had begun his political career. In 1782, Fauquier County, where he had grown up, elected him to the House of Delegates in the Virginia General Assembly. More significantly, when the assembly met, his fellow delegates, undoubtedly recognizing Marshall's unusual intellect and talent, elected him to the Governor's Privy Council, a body consisting largely of experienced state leaders, even though he was merely twenty-seven years old. In 1785, Marshall was elected an alderman of Richmond, his then place of residence, and his fellow aldermen then elected him recorder of the city, in which position he served for three years as a member of Richmond's municipal court, the Hustings Court.

Marshall's most important moments of public service in the 1780s came during the Virginia convention that had been called in 1788 to debate ratification of the proposed federal Constitution. Marshall was a key spokesman for the Federalist forces at the convention. The main task with which the Federalist leadership charged Marshall was the defense of the judiciary article of the Constitution and of the federal courts that, it was expected, Congress would create.

Marshall, in particular, tried to show that federal judges would be protectors of liberty rather than a threat to liberty. Most notably, he argued that the judiciary would guard against any attempt by Congress to enact legislation in excess of its delegated powers. As Marshall explained in anticipation of the *Marbury* decision some fifteen years later, if Congress "were to make a law not warranted by any of the powers enumerated, it would be considered by the judges as an infringement of the constitution which they were to guard. They would declare it void." Most historians have been of the view that

Marshall's speeches in support of the Constitution were helpful in persuading the majority of delegates who secured ratification of the new government on the part of Virginia.

In view of his ability, his ties to Washington, and his services at the Virginia ratifying convention, Marshall undoubtedly was eligible for office under the new federal regime. But he did not want it. Instead, Marshall began the 1790s earning a handsome income from his burgeoning law practice, investing the proceeds in the Fairfax estate and other western land speculations, and assisting friends and family, especially his father, in their land speculations. His ambition was not the national and ultimately international fame that eventually would come his way, but rather the establishment of a great family, like those of the Jeffersons, the Randolphs, and the Lees, to whom he was distantly related. In this ambition, he was typical of Virginians of his time.

Although he declined national office during the years of Washington's administration, Marshall nevertheless remained active in Virginia politics. From Virginia, he took strong stands in defense of President Washington and his administration, particularly of his foreign policy and of the treaty with England negotiated in 1794 by John Jay. His growing expertise on foreign affairs made him an obvious candidate for appointment to the three-man mission that President John Adams created in 1797 to negotiate a settlement to difficulties with the French Republic. Although he was unsure about accepting the assignment, Marshall ultimately decided to acquiesce out of an expectation that the mission would last only several months and that a brief absence would not interfere with his private law practice.

In the end, Marshall was absent from Virginia for slightly more than a year, and his efforts in Paris did not result in negotiation of a settlement. Nevertheless, the unsuccessful negotiation effort catapulted Marshall onto the national political stage as a hero.

Marshall's political success resulted from his superior understanding, which later would serve him well in his years as chief justice, of the workings of American democracy and constitutionalism. Upon meeting with French foreign minister Talleyrand, Marshall and his two fellow diplomats, who had come to negotiate issues regarding American neutrality and trade, were informed that the French government would not discuss those issues until the United States loaned $12 million to France and paid bribes totaling $250,000 to Talleyrand and other French officials. Perhaps Talleyrand did not appreciate what Marshall instinctively knew—that such sums could be paid only upon congressional appropriation and that the American people never would permit Congress to appropriate funds for what appeared to be bribes and tribute. (The sum of $12 million was a large one for 1798; all of the Louisiana Territory was purchased from France merely five years later for the slightly larger sum of $15 million.) Armed with this knowledge, Marshall set out simply to lay before the American public a clear record of his transactions in France; he understood, as he wrote at the time, that the "mass" of his fellow citizens required "no more than to understand a question to decide it properly." Thus, he refused the French demands, made a public record of his refusal, and returned home as a hero.

Marshall's reports contributed to the building of anti-French sentiment in the United States, but Marshall himself continued to counsel moderation. In particular, he reported to President John Adams that he did not believe France wanted war with the United States and that war should be avoided. In his view, the French would negotiate once they realized that the American people supported their president.

The reasons for Marshall's moderation are unclear. Perhaps he had merely read the French accurately and was reporting to Adams intelligence that he had gathered in Paris. Alternatively, Marshall may have been reading his own home base of Richmond, Virginia, accurately: he knew that Virginians distrusted John Adams, he may have feared that they would not follow Adams into war, and he therefore may have urged Adams to preserve the Union by avoiding a war that could have fractured it. A third possibility is that Marshall was instinctively a man of moderation who strove to avoid unnecessary strife and create consensus among potential adversaries; as we shall see when we come to *Marbury v. Madison*, Marshall again pursued a course of moderation in dealing with that case.

Upon the conclusion of his French mission and his return to Richmond, Marshall wanted only to return to private law practice and to tend to his pecuniary affairs. Partisan politics, however, were growing hotter, and John Marshall's mentor, former president George Washington, thought it essential to get good Federalists elected to

Congress. Accordingly, Washington summoned Marshall to Mount Vernon and informed him that it was his patriotic duty to run in the 1799 Virginia elections for Congress. Marshall ultimately performed his duty, as requested by Washington, and pursued a seat in Congress even after President Adams offered him a seat on the Supreme Court made vacant by the death of Justice James Wilson.

Marshall's campaign for Congress again illustrated his moderation, as well as his understanding of the workings of democratic politics. His key stand was his opposition to the Alien and Sedition Acts, which had been adopted by the Federalist Congress in order to make criminal and thereby stamp out newspaper criticism of the Adams administration but which had aroused strong resistance throughout the South, especially Virginia. Perhaps John Marshall thought it wrong to use the power of the national government against political opponents in the fashion authorized by the Alien and Sedition Acts, or perhaps he simply saw that he could not win election from his Richmond, Virginia, district unless he expressed opposition to the acts. For whatever reason, he was the only Federalist running for Congress who announced his opposition to the legislation, and he was one of the few Federalists who won election from the South.

Once he arrived at the nation's temporary capital of Philadelphia, Marshall's moderation and lawyerly skills made him one of the most important political leaders in town. The Federalist Speaker of the House, Theodore Sedgwick, reported that Marshall possessed "great powers" and "much dexterity in the application of them" and that the Federalists could "do nothing without him." As a freshman, he was one of five congressmen named to committees considering a national bankruptcy act and an act enlarging the federal judiciary. He played an especially important role in connection with the first act, when he sought to soften opposition to the measure with an amendment calling for a jury trial on any issues of fact; without Marshall's amendment, the bankruptcy bill would not have passed the House, and the Bankruptcy Act of 1800 never would have become law.

Marshall also became the leading spokesman for President Adams in connection with the Thomas Nash affair. Nash, who had been one of a band of British sailors who had mutinied and murdered their officers, had been captured in Charleston, South Carolina, and extradited to Britain pursuant to the Jay Treaty, even though he had claimed to be an American citizen. Adams's opponents in Congress argued that Nash should not have been extradited until his claim of American citizenship had been adjudicated in court. Marshall, in a speech on the floor of the House, responded that the federal judiciary lacked jurisdiction in the Nash affair since there was no case or controversy between individual parties subject to judicial process and amenable to orders of the court; the dispute was between two sovereigns, Great Britain and the United States. When Congressman Albert Gallatin rose to rebut Marshall, he conceded instead that Marshall's argument was correct. It should be noted that the Judiciary Act of 1789 had not given federal judges jurisdiction to issue writs of habeas corpus, the device that would be used today to obtain an adjudication of whether Nash could be lawfully turned over to British authorities.

Marshall's political stock rose even further when, as Congress was about to adjourn in May 1800, divisions among the Federalists shattered the party. More extreme members of the party, responding to the leadership of Alexander Hamilton, deserted the Adams administration and provided little support for the president's 1800 reelection campaign. As a result of the desertion, two positions in the cabinet—secretary of war and secretary of state—became vacant.

John Marshall was a member of the more moderate wing of the party, which remained loyal to President Adams. As a result, Adams brought Marshall into the administration, when on May 7, 1800, he named Marshall as the new secretary of war. Marshall, however, never assumed the office because five days later, on May 12, 1800, Adams named him secretary of state.

Marshall's main duty as secretary of state was to preside over the conduct of American foreign policy. In performing this duty, he adhered to his own and the president's policy of maintaining peace with both Britain and France and thus steered a middle course between factional groups in America desiring war with one or the other.

Marshall also had some important domestic duties. The most important was his superintendence of the federal government's move from Philadelphia to its permanent capital of Washington, DC. Another was drafting President Adams's final annual message to Congress in December 1800, in which Marshall included a plea for reform of the judiciary. Through his ten months in the cabinet,

John Marshall served as a trusted advisor to the president, who was in the midst of a reelection campaign against Thomas Jefferson and his Democratic-Republicans and who was also cut off from most of the leaders of his own Federalist Party, who regarded him as too moderate. Marshall was one of the few political figures who agreed with the policies of President Adams and was not eager to see the end of his term in office.

Nonetheless, despite his closeness to the president, John Marshall did not participate in the campaign of 1800. Instead, as we shall see, he preserved amicable relations with all sides, with the result that he had a pivotal role in postelectoral events during the winter of 1801.

As we saw in chapter 6, John Adams lost the 1800 presidential race, but Thomas Jefferson did not emerge as the undisputed winner. Instead, Jefferson found himself tied for the lead in electoral votes with Aaron Burr, his running mate. Since no one candidate had an undisputed majority in the Electoral College, the choice between the two leaders, Jefferson and Burr, was thrown to the House of Representatives, where Federalists held the balance of power.

Marshall knew Thomas Jefferson, who was a distant cousin, well and distrusted him greatly. Thus, it is not surprising that late in December 1800 Marshall wrote a letter to Charles Pinckney, the Federalist candidate for vice president, delicately suggesting to him that he use his influence with congressmen from his home state of South Carolina to persuade them to vote against Jefferson. Rumors abounded at the time of the letter that the Federalists would unite to prevent the election of any president or vice president, which would lead to a turnover of executive power to either the chief justice or the ranking cabinet member, the secretary of state. Since the office of chief justice was vacant when Marshall wrote his letter, rumor suggested that Marshall himself would have assumed executive powers and become acting president if the House of Representatives had failed to consummate the election.

The letter to Pinckney was uncharacteristic of Marshall, however, and did not indicate the role he would play during the winter of 1801. Far more typical was his response to a letter he received from Alexander Hamilton, the leader of the extreme wing of the Federalist Party, which had deserted President Adams and undercut his reelection bid. Hamilton had been the rival of Thomas Jefferson ever since they had served together in the first cabinet of President Washington, but his rivalry in New York politics with Aaron Burr was even more vicious. In Hamilton's view, Jefferson was the lesser of two evils as president, and Hamilton accordingly began a campaign to induce the House of Representatives to select Jefferson rather than Burr as president. As part of that campaign, Hamilton wrote a letter to Marshall, in which he stated his reasons for opposing Burr and urged Marshall to support Jefferson.

Marshall responded initially by noting his objections to Jefferson. Then, he conceded that if Hamilton's description of Burr was accurate, the choice of Burr would be an even greater mistake than the selection of Jefferson. Marshall concluded his response by observing that, in light of Hamilton's representations, he no longer could favor Burr, but that at the same time he could "not bring myself to aid Mr. Jefferson." Accordingly, Marshall promised Hamilton that he would take no part in the business of selecting the next president.

The available evidence, in fact, indicates that after writing his letter to Hamilton, Marshall took no further part in the political battles that ultimately led to Thomas Jefferson's election as president. Instead, he adopted an approach, which he would later bring to the American judiciary, of standing aside from political conflict, of doing his own work, and of letting the democratic political process take its own course. He remained neutral.

Marshall also left no evidence that he played any role in his own selection as chief justice, which occurred less than a month before the House of Representatives finally broke the Jefferson-Burr tie. The office of chief justice of the United States had become vacant when Oliver Ellsworth, the incumbent, became ill and in December 1800 submitted his resignation to President Adams. Adams initially offered the position to John Jay, who had been the first chief justice and was a loyal Federalist and a lawyer and statesman of distinction. However, Jay, who had once resigned from the job, declined reappointment and, in January 1801, so informed the president.

At that point, two sitting justices appeared to be the most obvious candidates for the office. One was William Cushing, the senior associate justice and an old colleague of Adams from Massachusetts in times before and during the War of Independence, when they had both been lawyers and judges. The other was William Paterson of

New Jersey, who had been a leading figure at the 1787 Constitutional Convention and later a senator from his state. The objection to Cushing was his age, which was sixty-nine; the objection to Paterson was Adams's unwillingness to prefer him over his old friend Cushing as well as Paterson's support for the Hamilton wing of the Federalist Party rather than for Adams in the election of 1800.

Marshall himself supported the appointment of Paterson, and when he presented Adams with Jay's letter declining appointment, he proposed Paterson's name. But Adams responded in no uncertain terms that he would not appoint Paterson. It was also clear that Cushing's age barred his appointment. The result was that Adams was in a bind. Less than six weeks remained in his administration. If Adams failed to appoint a new chief justice, Thomas Jefferson or Aaron Burr would make the appointment, and the Federalists' opportunity to dominate the Supreme Court during the years to come would lapse. Adams did not have time to canvass the nation by the slow mails of 1801 to determine whether leading Federalists wished to assume the office. He had to offer the chief justiceship to someone close at hand who would either accept it or reject it quickly enough so that he could then offer it to someone else.

As the secretary of state in the Adams administration, John Marshall was close at hand. Adams also knew of Marshall's intelligence and general level of ability, as well as his loyalty to Adams's vision of Federalism and his political moderation. Accordingly, Adams nominated Marshall.

Marshall immediately accepted, but the Federalists in Congress were astounded. Marshall was young (only forty-five years of age at the time) and had rebelled against party discipline, and his appointment meant that older, more distinguished, and more reliable Federalists were being passed over. For this reason, the Senate delayed confirmation of Marshall for a week. But, although some Federalists remained hesitant even though only five weeks remained in the Adams administration, the choice of John Marshall as chief justice of the United States was finally confirmed by the Senate, in part because of the enthusiastic support of all fifteen Jeffersonian Republicans, who admired Marshall's rebellions against party discipline as well as his general moderation. On February 4, 1801—precisely one month before Thomas Jefferson was sworn in as president—Marshall took his seat as chief justice. Little business was conducted during the 1801 term, however, and no decisions were handed down.

Meanwhile, at Adams's request, Marshall remained on for the final month of the administration as the acting secretary of state. As such, he became actively involved in the transfer of power from Adams to Jefferson once it became clear in mid-February 1801 that Jefferson would be the next president. Thus, he advised American diplomats overseas to delay engaging in negotiations or making other decisions that might bind the new Jefferson administration to policies it might not accept.

Marshall also sought to move beyond the harsh rhetoric of the electoral campaign and to restore greater civility to relationships between the two political parties. Thus, when Jefferson informed Marshall that he had no one to help him prepare the various messages he would need to give at the outset of his administration, Marshall promptly assigned the chief clerk of the State Department to work with the president-elect.

Both Jefferson and Marshall recognized the importance of a peaceful, orderly transition of power after the hotly fought 1800 election. Such a transition had never occurred before in American history, and Jefferson and Marshall worked together to bring it about. Whatever Marshall's fears of Jefferson may have been as late as December 1800, Marshall was willing to give Jefferson the benefit of the doubt in the days before his inauguration and to anticipate that the "public prosperity and happiness" would "sustain no diminution under democratic guidance." Although Marshall continued to distrust some of Jefferson's partisan supporters, he indicated in a letter written on inauguration day that he did not distrust the president-elect himself.

Thus, when Jefferson requested Marshall to administer the presidential oath of office at noon on March 4, 1801, Marshall promptly agreed. He appears to have appreciated fully the symbolic significance of having the highest-ranking officeholder of the outgoing Federalist Party, which he became when John Adams left Washington, DC, on the morning of the inauguration, swear in the new president as the leader of the opposing Democratic-Republican Party. Jefferson, in turn, reciprocated by delivering a conciliatory inaugural address and by asking Marshall to remain on as secretary of state for a few extra days until James Madison, his successor, arrived in town.

Thus, it is essential to understand that, as John Marshall assumed the bench following one of the most ferocious political fights in American history, he was no fanatic. On the contrary, he was a moderate who understood the importance of allowing the democratic political process to follow its course. His goal was to bring people together and to restore harmony and consensus, not to divide them further and thereby lead them to violence and bloodshed. It is against the background of this moderation that we must understand *Marbury v. Madison*, the landmark opinion that Marshall delivered only two years after his ascension to the bench and Jefferson's assumption of the presidency.

CHAPTER EIGHT

Marbury and the Crisis of 1801–1803

Although Jefferson and Marshall behaved in a conciliatory fashion toward each other in an effort to effectuate a peaceful transition of power on March 4, 1801, other Federalists and Republicans remained more partisan. Among the more partisan were the Federalist leaders of the lame-duck Congress that met in December 1800 and promptly enacted the Judiciary Act of 1801, which revamped the lower federal judiciary. The act expanded the jurisdiction of the federal courts and created a number of new federal judgeships, which President Adams, in his closing days in office, filled entirely with Federalists, who came to be known as midnight judges, from the belated nature of their appointments.

To appreciate the significance of the 1801 act, it is necessary to focus on the role of federal courts in the constitutional order. Unlike government today, late eighteenth- and early nineteenth-century government still did not possess a large bureaucracy capable of enforcing the law and bringing its will to bear on local communities. Judges constituted the principal body of officials through whom central governing authorities could have a presence in localities.

Under the Articles of Confederation, no federal courts had existed, except for a Court of Appeals in Admiralty Cases, which had reviewed several state trial court judgments, all of them involving the capture of British vessels by American privateers during the course of the War for Independence. All other cases involving national law or national policy began and ended in the state courts, with no possibility of appeal to any national court.

Thus, the Confederation Congress, in effect, was totally dependent on state judges to enforce national law, and it was easy to anticipate, if national law and state policy were inconsistent, that state judges would not enforce national law, such as the rule proclaimed by the peace treaty that had ended the Revolutionary War that British creditors would suffer no impediments to the collection of their debts. Americans seeking a strong national government, either on general principles or in order to enforce specific national policies—and nearly all members of the Federalist Party in 1800 fit within either the one or the other category—therefore sought the creation of federal courts, preferably with original as well as appellate jurisdiction, to perform the task, as no other institution could, of enforcing national policies.

The Philadelphia Convention reached a compromise when it drafted the Constitution itself in 1787. The convention mandated the creation of a Supreme Court, to which litigants in either state courts or lower federal courts could take an appeal in any case involving federal law. The Supreme Court, however, possesses only limited power to enforce national law, since many litigants will be unable to appeal cases to it, and even when appeals are taken, lower courts will not always enforce the Supreme Court's mandates. Lower federal courts thus are essential to effective enforcement of national law, but in respect to lower courts, the Philadelphia Convention compromised, as it left to future Congresses decisions about whether to create any lower federal courts and, if it created them, about the scope of their jurisdiction.

Even with this compromise, however, Americans who began to style themselves Anti-Federalists were troubled by the provisions of the Constitution dealing with the judiciary, and they levied attacks on those provisions during the ratification debates. Anti-Federalists worried that federal courts posed a threat to local liberties. Familiar with a world in which state-court judges and law-finding juries had power to block the enforcement of national policies in any locality that did not accept them, the Anti-Federalists feared that Congress might create federal courts in which judges had power to determine the outcome of cases; such federal courts would weaken the power of the states to nullify federal policy.

The Bill of Rights responded, in part, to these Anti-Federalist concerns—especially to concerns that juries might be weakened or even eliminated from a new federal judicial system. First, the Seventh Amendment guaranteed the right to trial by jury in all civil cases at law in which the amount in controversy exceeded twenty dollars.

Second, the right to jury trial in criminal cases, which had been preserved in the original Constitution, was further protected in the Sixth Amendment by the guarantee that the jury would be drawn from the district wherein the alleged crime had been committed. Third, the Bill of Rights guaranteed that no fact found by a jury could be reexamined by a judge, except to the extent allowed at common law.

But the Bill of Rights constituted a compromise rather than a capitulation to Anti-Federalist demands. The Sixth and Seventh Amendments protected the control of juries over fact-finding, but they did not place the power of juries to find law beyond change by Congress or the judiciary. Thus, the amendments left open the possibility that a powerful federal judiciary could overturn jury nullification of federal law and thereby enforce federal policies in recalcitrant states.

The First Congress continued the policy of compromise in its decisions regarding the creation of a national judiciary. The Judiciary Act of 1789 established only a meager federal judiciary and gave it only limited jurisdiction, in particular over cases between litigants from different states. The 1789 act did not, however, give jurisdiction over all matters of federal law to the federal courts. Moreover, it created only two sorts of judges, Supreme Court judges and district judges, and it provided that federal circuit courts, which were granted most of the jurisdiction conferred by the act, would consist of one district judge and two Supreme Court judges riding circuit. Since each Supreme Court judge might be required to sit on circuit courts in at least five different locations, the 1789 act guaranteed that the principal federal trial courts could meet only infrequently and could not rival state judges and state juries as institutions for resolution of the great mass of legal disputes. Finally, the act allowed most civil litigants to bring cases to federal courts only when they were seeking a judgment of at least five hundred dollars—a large amount for 1789 and an amount that ensured that most Americans would never be summoned into a federal court as a defendant.

Thus, when the lame-duck Federalist Congress assembled in December 1800, it met against the background of over a decade of conflict about the existence, size, and jurisdiction of the federal judiciary—conflict that had been resolved through compromises that had created a meager and somewhat inconsequential system of federal courts. The Judiciary Act of 1801 upset these compromises. It gave federal courts jurisdiction to hear all cases involving questions of federal law and, in addition, lowered, from five hundred to one hundred dollars the minimum amount of money that a plaintiff had to claim in order to bring a federal suit.

As a result of these changes, many more Americans could have been summoned into federal courts. Moreover, the 1801 act made those courts more efficient. In particular, it created sixteen new circuit judges, who collectively would have had a substantially greater capacity to determine lawsuits than the six Supreme Court judges who had been riding circuit under the 1789 act.

The midnight judges appointed by President Adams only exacerbated the concerns of those opposed to expanding the federal courts. The Judiciary Act of 1801 became law on February 13—less than three weeks before John Adams's term as president expired. Undaunted, however, Adams managed to appoint and obtain Senate confirmation for sixteen new circuit judges, all of them Federalists, as well as for several judges of courts, newly created by an act of February 27, 1801, in the District of Columbia. Unfortunately, Secretary of State Marshall was unable to deliver the commission for one of the new justices of the peace for the district, a certain William Marbury, before the end of President Adams's term, and James Madison, the new secretary of state, refused to make the uncompleted delivery. Upon his refusal, Marbury brought a suit for a writ of mandamus against Madison in the Supreme Court, and thus the case of *Marbury v. Madison* began. A writ of mandamus (which obtains its name from the Latin verb *mandamus*, which in translation means "we order") is a document issued by a court that orders a defendant, in this case Secretary of State Madison, to perform a specified act, in this case to deliver a commission, on behalf of a specified plaintiff, in this case William Marbury.

But, before the Court could hear the case, Congress, now under the control of the Jeffersonian Republicans, intervened and passed the Judiciary Act of 1802, which repealed the Judiciary Act of 1801. Cases pending in the new circuit courts established under the 1801 act were transferred by the 1802 legislation back to the old circuit courts that had existed under the 1789 act. Congress also postponed the next term of the Supreme Court until 1803 so that the Court could not rule on the constitutionality of the 1802 act before the act went into effect.

Nonetheless, in one case so transferred, *Stuart v. Laird*, the defendant argued that the 1802 repeal act, and hence the transfer of his case, was unconstitutional. When his argument was rejected in the lower court, he appealed to the Supreme Court. Decided only six days after *Marbury*, *Stuart* became, in effect, a companion case in determining the legitimacy of the judicial policies of both Federalists and Republicans during the transition from the Adams to the Jefferson administration.

Marbury v. Madison and *Stuart v. Laird*, both decided in 1803, thus created the possibility of a direct confrontation between the Federalist judiciary left over from the Adams administration and the new Jeffersonian Congress. In such a confrontation, Congress would have been very much on the offensive. As one Republican newspaper, the *Boston Independent Chronicle*, warned in 1803, any attempt "of federalism to exalt the Judiciary over the Executive and Legislature, and to give that favorite department a political character & influence" would "terminate in the degradation and disgrace of the judiciary." However, Chief Justice Marshall, by nature a compromiser, was not inclined to take up this Republican challenge and generate a clash with President Jefferson and his Republican Congress.

John Marshall had no propensity to turn *Marbury* and *Stuart* into instances of judicial review of the sort that the Jeffersonians feared. Although Chief Justice Marshall was prepared, as he wrote, to "disregard" the pressures of partisan politics when they were "put in competition with . . . his duty" to uphold the law and always kept in mind the desirability of adjudicating at least some matters by a nonmajoritarian standard and thereby restraining "the capricious *will* of the rulers of the day," he and his fellow Federalist justices, with the possible exception of Justice Samuel Chase, were not elitist antidemocrats. They appreciated the need to steer clear of partisan controversy and not to challenge unnecessarily legislation enacted by democratic majorities. As Marshall's private correspondence with his colleagues in the opening years of the 1800s indicates, the chief justice and his colleagues were fully aware of "the consequences of refusing to carry . . . into effect" a law enacted by a popular majority.

Marshall and the other justices, in short, strove to reconcile popular will and legal principle, not to make one either superior or subservient to the other. They had no intention to behave as the Supreme Court ultimately would in *Cooper v. Aaron*, a 1958 school desegregation case in which the Court for the first time in its history explicitly arrogated to itself the exclusive power to interpret the Constitution. Unlike the justices in *Cooper*, Marshall and his colleagues did not declare themselves to be the ultimate arbiters of the nation's constitutional policy choices, with power to bind coordinate branches of government to their judgments of constitutionality and thereby invalidate popularly supported legislative policies inconsistent with the constitutional values they favored. *Marbury v. Madison* and *Stuart v. Laird* would be much narrower decisions.

John Marshall and the other Federalist justices achieved their narrow goals in *Marbury* and *Stuart* by distinguishing between the domain of law and the domain of politics. Indeed, the foundation of Marshall's constitutional jurisprudence is the distinction between political matters, to be resolved by the legislative and executive branches in the new democratic, majoritarian style, and legal matters, to be resolved by the judiciary in the style of government by consensus and fixed principles that had prevailed in most eighteenth-century American courts. Marshall, of course, invented neither style, nor did he first apply the latter to the adjudicatory process. His creative act was to use the distinction between law and politics to circumscribe, however imperfectly, the extent to which the political, majoritarian style could engulf all government, as it was threatening in 1800 to do.

Merely announcing a line between law and politics does not, of course, fully differentiate the legal from the political. It is also necessary to put content into the line by articulating consistent and precise criteria for identifying matters appropriately decided by the legal method. We need to examine both *Marbury v. Madison* and *Stuart v. Laird* in considerable detail to appreciate how John Marshall and his fellow justices accomplished this difficult task.

Marshall began the *Marbury* opinion with a narrow and technical ruling—that President Adams's signature on Marbury's commission completed Marbury's appointment to the office of justice of the peace and entitled him to the delivery of his commission. This ruling was especially important, however, because for most lawyers of Marshall's generation a right to an office was analogous to a right to land or other property. It meant that Marbury possessed "a vested legal right" to his commission, and it led the chief justice to the second issue in his opinion—whether Marbury had a remedy for the deprivation of the right.

When summoned before the Court in the preliminary stages of the case, Department of State officers had claimed not only that Marbury had no remedy for the delivery of his commission, but also that they were privileged, by virtue of their executive status, not to testify about any transactions concerning the commission. Marshall recognized this as a potentially far-reaching claim, for if the government asserted such a privilege in matters involving land patents, which Marshall and lawyers of his time, as we have seen, thought analogous to commissions for office, it would cloud the title to much of the land west of the Appalachians. Unfounded fears had intensified the political divisions of 1800, and, whatever the truth may have been, the Federalist Court doubtless feared that Thomas Jefferson's new administration might claim to be above the law in these matters as well as others. Marshall's real difficulty was that he, unlike more extreme Federalists, could not summarily reject the claim of executive privilege, for as he had once told his constituents, he believed that the people, and hence their agents in the political branches of government, must sometimes be free to act unbound by fixed legal principles.

Accordingly, his central task in *Marbury* was to specify when law bound the political branches and when it did not. To do so, he and the Court distinguished between political matters, such as foreign policy, as to which the legislature and executive were accountable only to the electorate, on the one hand, and trifling administrative matters and matters of individual right, on the other, which the courts would protect by adhering to established rules and fixed principles. In Marshall's own words, "political" subjects "respect[ed] the nation, not individual rights" and were governed by a political branch whose decisions were "never . . . examinable by the courts" but "only politically examinable."

In contrast, there were cases where "a specific duty [was] assigned by law, and individual rights depend[ed] upon the performance of that duty." In such cases involving "the rights of individuals," every officer of government was "amenable to the laws for his conduct;

and [could not] at his discretion sport away . . . vested rights," and a person such as Marbury who possessed a vested right was entitled to a remedy. In Marshall's own words, "the very essence of civil liberty certainly consist[ed] in the right of every individual to claim the protection of the laws, whenever he receives an injury." The same was true in regard to procedural rules for administering courts and other institutions and for adjudicating disputes.

Thus, William Marbury was entitled to some remedy for deprivation of his right to office. But was he entitled to the particular remedy he had sought—a writ of mandamus issued by the Supreme Court of the United States in a suit commenced before it? The Judiciary Act of 1789 authorized the Court to issue writs of mandamus, but the judiciary article of the Constitution presented a problem, in that it limited the original jurisdiction of the Supreme Court to specified categories of cases, of which mandamus was not one. In order for the Court to issue the writ, it thus would have to reach one of two conclusions: either that Congress had power to grant original jurisdiction to the Supreme Court in cases in which the Constitution denied it or that an action for mandamus in the Supreme Court was not the commencement of an original proceeding but a form of appeal from the official against whom the writ was being sought.

It is noteworthy that Marbury's counsel did not press the argument that by granting mandamus in a suit commenced before it the Supreme Court exercised its original jurisdiction over original matters not specified in the Constitution. Instead, he mainly argued that the Court exercised appellate jurisdiction when issuing mandamus in a proceeding commenced before it. According to the thrust of his argument, which flowed from an accurate reading of *Federalist No. 81*, "the word 'appellate' [was] not to be taken in its technical sense, . . . but in its broadest sense, in which it denotes nothing more than the power of one tribunal" to have "by reason of its supremacy . . . the superintendence of . . . inferior tribunals and officers, whether judicial or ministerial." In 1803, when the concept of appeal had not yet assumed its relatively narrow and precise modern meaning, that argument was plausible, and a court anxious to grant Marbury relief could easily have accepted it.

Plainly, the issue whether a proceeding for mandamus was an original or appellate matter was not a matter of politics, but a matter of judicial administration within the special expertise of judges. Marshall so treated it and rejected the argument of Marbury's counsel. To have accepted the argument would have contradicted Marshall's distinction between matters of political discretion and matters of legal right, for it would have frequently led the Court to "revis[e] and correct the proceedings in a cause already instituted" in the executive branch and might thereby have brought before the Court all the issues, of both law, fact, and politics, that the executive branch had previously considered. Such review might have continually presented the Court with political questions of executive motive. To avoid this danger and to ensure that the court serve as the purely legal institution he envisioned, Marshall had to consider a mandamus against officials, as distinguished from a mandamus against lower court judges, as an original action in which the court granting the writ could confine the action's scope to properly legal rather than political matters. Thus, he had to reject the claim that mandamus was a direct appeal from the executive to the Supreme Court.

That brought Chief Justice Marshall to the issue of whether Congress could grant the Supreme Court jurisdiction that the Constitution denied it. Note how, so far in his opinion, Marshall and his fellow justices had underscored the distinction between law and politics. They had held, as did most then existing case law, that once the president appointed Marbury to a judicial office, Marbury had a property right in that office and was entitled to a legal remedy through which to enforce the right. They also had ruled that an appeal from the secretary of state's refusal to deliver Marbury's commission was the wrong remedy, since such an appeal would have brought the discretionary political concerns that had prompted the secretary's refusal before the Court and thus would have embroiled the Court in a political rather than purely legal matter.

But how could Marshall and his fellow justices complete their *Marbury* opinion without exercising political judgment and thereby becoming entangled in politics? To grant an original writ of mandamus directing Secretary of State Madison to put Marbury in office would have forced a confrontation between the Court and the Jefferson administration, which could have ended at best with Madison's refusal to obey the Court's order and at worst with Congress's impeachment of Chief Justice John Marshall and his subsequent conviction and removal from office. Thus, Marshall had to find a way to deny Marbury the writ of mandamus he was seeking. The way he found was to declare unconstitutional Congress's grant of jurisdiction to the Court, in the Judiciary Act of 1789, to issue original writs of mandamus. This recourse to judicial review, however, strikes readers at the outset of the twenty-first century as perhaps even more political than granting the writ to Marbury would have been.

But Marshall did not understand judicial review as we do today. For Marshall and his colleagues on the Supreme Court, judicial review neither required nor permitted judges to exercise political discretion. In that familiar portion of the *Marbury* opinion that asserts the power of judicial review, Marshall reiterated his belief in "the fundamental principles" of law that were "designed to be permanent." But at no point in the opinion did he invoke the language of natural rights, nor did he rely on precedent or other prior judicial authority. In fact, he cited only one case in his entire opinion. In short, Marshall never relied upon principles that either were made by or required interpretation by judges. On the contrary, the principles that he found fundamental acquired their authority from the "original right" of the people "to establish, for their future government, such principles as, in their opinion, shall most conduce to their own happiness." In so ruling, the Marshall Court evoked the Revolutionary generation's assumption that the people, acting as a unitary body rather than as disparate individuals, had incorporated basic and generally agreed upon principles of right into their Constitution. The Court thereby reverted to something like the governance by consensus techniques of its eighteenth-century predecessors.

For Marshall and his colleagues, judicial review merely required comparison of fixed and unchanging fundamental principles incorporated by a consensus of the people into the written text of the Constitution, which in the case of *Marbury* conferred original jurisdiction on the Supreme Court only in specified categories of cases and declared its jurisdiction to be appellate in all other cases, with the text of legislation, which gave the Court original jurisdiction over a category not within the Constitution's specifications. As the *Marbury* opinion declared, it was emphatically the province and duty of the judicial department to say what the law is. . . . If two laws conflict[ed] with each other, the courts must decide on the operation of each.

So if a law be in opposition to the constitution; if both the law and the constitution apply to a particular case, so that the court must either decide that case conformably to the law, disregarding the constitution; or conformably to the constitution, disregarding the law; the court must determine which of these conflicting rules governs the case. This is of the very essence of judicial duty.

If then, . . . the constitution is superior to any ordinary act of the legislature, the constitution, and not such ordinary act, must govern the case to which they both apply.

Those then who controvert the principle that the constitution is to be considered, in court, as a paramount law, are reduced to the necessity of maintaining that courts must close their eyes on the constitution, and see only the law.

This doctrine would subvert the very foundation of all written constitutions. It would declare that an act which, according to the principles and theory of our government, is entirely void, is yet, in practice, completely obligatory. It would declare that if the legislature shall do what is expressly forbidden, such act, notwithstanding the express prohibition, is in reality effectual. It would be giving to the legislature a practical and real omnipotence, with the same breath which professes to restrict their powers within narrow limits. It is prescribing limits, and declaring that those limits may be passed at pleasure.

That it thus reduces to nothing what we have deemed the greatest improvement on political institutions—a written constitution—. . . [is] sufficient, in America, where written constitutions have been viewed with so much reverence[,] for rejecting the construction.

The Supreme Court's approach in *Marbury v. Madison* was not new, of course; *Federalist No. 78* had formulated it much earlier. There Alexander Hamilton had written: "Some perplexity respecting the right of the courts to pronounce legislative acts void, because contrary to the constitution, has arisen from an imagination that the doctrine would imply a superiority of the judiciary to the legislative power. It is urged that the authority which can declare the acts of another void, must necessary be superior to the one whose acts may be declared void."

But, Hamilton continued, it would be wrong so to imply judicial superiority. On the contrary, it was

> far more rational to suppose that the courts were designed to be an intermediate body between the people and the legislature, in order, among other things, to keep the latter within the limits assigned to their authority. The interpretation of the laws is the proper and peculiar function of the courts. A constitution is in fact, and must be, regarded by the judges as a fundamental law. It therefore belongs to them to ascertain its meaning as well as the meaning of any particular act proceeding from the legislative body. If there should happen to be an irreconcilable variance between the two, that which has the superior obligation and validity ought of course to be preferred; or in other words, the constitution ought to be preferred to the statute, the intention of the people to the intention of their agents.
>
> Nor does this conclusion by any means suppose of superiority of the judicial to the legislative power. It only supposes that the power of the people is superior to both; and that where the will of the legislature declared in its statutes, stands in opposition to that of the people declared in the constitution, the judges ought to be governed by the latter, rather than the former. They ought to regulate their decisions by the fundamental laws, rather than by those which are not fundamental.

Hamilton, in turn, was merely following ideas that had been expressed earlier by delegates at the Constitutional Convention or elsewhere during the ratification debates. Thus, Luther Martin, a delegate from Maryland, had noted at the Philadelphia Convention that, "as to the Constitutionality of laws, that point will come before the Judges . . . [, and] they will have a negative on the laws," while Patrick Henry, the leader of the antiratification forces in Virginia, had declared during that state's ratification debates that it was "the highest encomium of this country, that the acts of the legislature, if unconstitutional, are liable to be opposed by the judiciary." Clearest of all had been Elbridge Gerry, a delegate from Massachusetts, who had taken note at Philadelphia of the judiciary's "power of deciding on the . . . constitutionality" of laws. "In some states," as Gerry accurately reported, "the judges had actually set aside laws as being against the Constitution. This was done too with general approbation."

Indeed, John Marshall himself had written during the 1780s of certain "maxims of democracy," which ought to be enforced by judges and which included "[a] strict observance of justice and public faith, and a steady adherence to virtue." And, during the Virginia ratification convention, as we have seen, Marshall had warned that if Congress "were to make a law not warranted by any of the powers enumerated, it would be considered by the Judges as an infringement of the Constitution which they are to guard:—They would not consider such a law as coming under their jurisdiction.—They would declare it void."

Of course, the propriety of exercising the power of judicial review was not without doubt prior to *Marbury v. Madison*. Opposition to judicial review has arisen in some states, most notably Rhode Island, after judges had utilized the power, and Hamilton had found it necessary to write *Federalist No. 78* precisely because a leading Anti-Federalist, Robert Yates, had plausibly warned that judges who made political judgments in the exercise of judicial review would in fact become policymakers with practical superiority over the legislature.

Still, whatever ambiguity may have existed, the Marshall Court's assumption of the power of judicial review was hardly unprecedented. Some forty cases had considered the doctrine in the four decades since James Otis had first articulated it, and many of those cases had adopted it. Chief Justice Marshall did nothing new when he relied on it. What was new was Marshall's commitment to use the power of judicial review only to preserve the rule of law in those cases where law was applicable, but never to enable the Court to assume policy-making powers. What was new was the chief justice's assurance that the Court would consider only legal and not political questions and his struggle, in those portions of the *Marbury* opinion that we now tend to ignore, to articulate a standard that would minimize the Court's political involvement.

Thus, the distinction between legal and political decision making runs throughout the *Marbury* opinion and is essential to understanding the case. It explains, for example, how Marshall could plausibly believe that judicial review involved not an exercise of political discretion by the Court, but merely a juxtaposing of statute with Constitution to see if they conflicted. When the Court could resolve a case according to established rules of procedure or seemingly fixed, consensus principles rather than transient policies, Marshall believed judicial review fell on the law side of the distinction and involved merely the judiciary's judicial protection of established practice and immutable, individual rights. In contrast, a case that required the Court to choose among transient policies or otherwise to exercise political discretion was not in Marshall's estimation an appropriate case for judicial review.

The distinction between law and politics outlined in *Marbury* gained force six days later from the Court's disposition of the other case pending before the Court that questioned the constitutionality of an act of Congress. *Stuart v. Laird* passed upon the Republicans' Judiciary Act of 1802, which repealed the Federalists' Judiciary Act of 1801.

Federalists had contended in Congress that the 1802 act was unconstitutional because it deprived judges appointed under the 1801 act of the lifetime tenure guaranteed by Article III, Section 1, of the Constitution. The 1802 act was also said to be unconstitutional because it required Supreme Court justices to sit as trial judges in circuit courts, thereby conferring an original jurisdiction that, the argument contended, only the Constitution could confer. *Marbury*, we ought to recall, had been decided on a somewhat analogous ground.

Nonetheless, the Marshall Court sustained the 1802 act. The apparent inconsistency between *Marbury* and *Stuart*, however, masks a deeper consistency in the Court's approach. Significantly, the court in *Stuart* never faced the contention that would have most troubled it: that the 1802 act unconstitutionally deprived judges of a right to hold office. That contention would have involved issues of legally enforceable private rights, but it was not even raised, for Stuart was not one of the judges deprived of office; he was merely a litigant objecting to the transfer of his case from a court constituted under the 1801 act to a court constituted under the 1802 act. His complaint raised no issue of fundamental private rights, only issues of Congress's political power to organize the lower federal courts.

There were two such issues. First, could Congress require a litigant to pursue his remedies in one court rather than another? As Marshall would suggest twenty-four years later in *Ogden v. Saunders*, the legislature clearly could control remedies. Second, could Congress require Supreme Court justices to ride circuit and thereby exercise an original jurisdiction not enumerated in the Constitution?

Marbury had decided, of course, that Congress could not expand the Supreme Court's original jurisdiction, but *Stuart* could be distinguished from *Marbury*, in that the 1802 Judiciary Act required individual justices, not the full Court, to exercise original jurisdiction. Further, as Justice Paterson explained for the unanimous Court, the 1802 act merely confirmed "practice and acquiescence" by Supreme Court justices "commencing with the organization of the judicial system." Such practice and acquiescence "afford[ed] an irresistible answer" to the claim of unconstitutionality; it was a "practical exposition . . . too strong and obstinate to be shaken or controlled," and "indeed fixed the construction" of the Constitution. The fact that the justices had performed the circuit duties imposed under the 1789 Judiciary Act put "the question . . . at rest." In *Marbury*, on the other hand, no strong public sentiment, precedent, or established practice stood in the way of holding that the Constitution's language prohibited the issuance of mandamus as a matter of original jurisdiction.

But a still more fundamental fact distinguished *Marbury* from *Stuart*. By invalidating the Republican-sponsored Judiciary Act of 1802, the Marshall Court would have embroiled itself in a political contest with Congress and the president that it might not have survived. If the Court was to withdraw from politics, as Marshall had said in *Marbury* it would, it had to capitulate to legislative judgments upon such politically controversial issues as the constitutionality of the 1802 act.

Accordingly, the Court sustained the act. By contrast, the only way to avoid the politics behind *Marbury* had been to construe the Constitution in a way to which few would object and thereby invalidate section 13 of the 1789 Judiciary Act. To have issued a writ of mandamus to James Madison as secretary of state would have thrust the Court into a political crisis. The Court's only other option—to hold on substantive grounds that Marbury had no right to the mandamus—would have denied some individuals access to the courts to enforce their legal rights. In short, to maintain Marshall's compromise—that courts would protect legal rights but refrain from adjudicating political questions—the Court had to decide both *Marbury* and *Stuart* as it did.

Thus, in two of the earliest cases decided by the Supreme Court following the 1800 election, Chief Justice John Marshall and the other Federalist justices on the Court publicly addressed the task of reconciling popular will, which had provided the basis for the Jeffersonian-Republican victory in the election, and immutable principles and established procedures, in which they, as well as many fellow citizens, continued to place their faith. As such, *Marbury* and *Stuart* were central to the process of differentiating law from politics, of declaring that the Supreme Court would abstain from the exercise of political judgment, and of making the preservation of the rule of law the Supreme Court's paradigmatic duty.

Although many historians will disagree, I remain convinced that judicial review was able to take root as progenitor of the rule of law in early nineteenth-century America because Marshall and his contemporaries believed, at some level, that the principles underlying constitutional government were nonpolitical—that is, that those principles existed independently of the will of the judges who applied them as well as the will of the political actors who flouted them. Of course, their belief was largely unarticulated, since they found its articulation as difficult as we find it to spell out our comparable beliefs. But at the same time that the principles underlying *Marbury* were largely unarticulated, they also were unproblematic because political elites, the only people who discussed such issues, accepted the justices' views. When elements of the elite did not agree with the Marshall Court's views, as, for instance, on issues of the scope of federal and state powers, the Court refused to act in an independent political fashion and to impose its own views but merely enforced the legislation that had been adopted by the majority of the Congress.

It is essential to emphasize, however, that by eschewing independent political decision making, the Court did not entirely remove itself from the political process. Cases as politically controversial as *Marbury* and *Stuart* still continued to find their way onto the Supreme Court's docket, and the Court continued to decide them. The justices also continued to behave strategically, as Marshall had in *Marbury*, where in dictum he proclaimed the Court's authority to enforce the law and lectured the president for violating it and then turned to the less controversial doctrine of judicial review as the foundation for a judgment acceptable both to the president and to Congress. But until it invalidated the Missouri Compromise in *Scott v. Sandford* some fifty-four years after *Marbury*, the Court never struck down a legislative policy judgment for which a substantial nationwide political majority had voted and to which many voters in the polity still adhered. In that final sense, the Marshall Court in *Marbury v. Madison* took itself out of politics.

CHAPTER NINE

The Early Impact of *Marbury*

For several decades after *Marbury v. Madison*, the assumptions of Chief Justice Marshall and his fellow justices about the nonpolitical character of judicial review provided an adequate foundation for the practice in state courts as well as the Supreme Court. As we shall see in this chapter, judicial review was uncontroversial in the early nineteenth century.

As soon as the Supreme Court had handed down its decisions in *Marbury v. Madison* and *Stuart v. Laird*, most political observers recognized the importance of the two cases. Both Federalist and Republican newspapers took note of the decisions and apprised readers of their significance. Some newspapers even published the *Marbury* opinion verbatim. On the whole, the politically active segments of the American public fully understood John Marshall's efforts at compromise. Although President Jefferson in later years would privately criticize the *Marbury* decision, he did not criticize it at the time the decision came down. Likewise, there was no criticism from Congress, which happened to be in session at the time of the decision. Similarly the Republican press, while giving extensive coverage to the decision, refrained from attacking it, while the Federalist press was, of course, supportive. Although the Marshall Court would later decide contentious issues and become engulfed in controversy, there was a general consensus that the Court had correctly decided both *Marbury v. Madison* and *Stuart v. Laird*. Only the political fringes of the Jeffersonian and Federalist parties had any doubts about the two decisions.

Why, we need to ask, did *Marbury* and *Stuart* seem so important and at the same time generate so little controversy? Several explanations come to the surface. First, the *Marbury* and *Stuart* decisions were modest ones that withdrew the courts from politics rather than inserting judges into the political maelstrom. Second, the implicit appeal to consensus in *Marbury* proved attractive to most early nineteenth-century Americans, who viewed political parties with foreboding and looked back fondly upon the more nonpartisan days of the eighteenth century. Third, the doctrine of judicial review, which *Marbury* proclaimed, was not novel: it went back forty years, and many state courts already had adopted it or soon would do so. Fourth, the idea of turning to law as the protector of private property—an idea at the core of John Marshall's jurisprudence—appealed to politically active Americans, most of whom either owned private property or expected to own it at some point in their lives.

At the heart of *Marbury v. Madison* was Chief Justice Marshall's withdrawal of the Supreme Court from partisan politics. Throughout the closing decades of eighteenth century, courts in America, on occasion, had been active formulators and enforcers of political policies. Judges had been active, some on the Tory but most on the Whig side, during the constitutional crisis eventuating in the War for Independence, and they remained active in the debtor-creditor and religious conflicts in various states after independence had been achieved. During the dozen years of the Washington and Adams presidencies, federal judges similarly had been active partisans of Federalist causes. President Washington had appointed only Federalists as judges, and once they had ascended the bench, they actively supported the policies of the two administrations, especially the efforts in the Adams years to repress political dissent through common law prosecutions for seditious libel and through enforcement of the Alien and Sedition Acts. The Judiciary Act of 1801 and the appointment exclusively of Federalists to the positions created under the act further injected the judiciary into the partisan strife of the preceding decade.

Arch-Federalists sought in *Marbury v. Madison* and *Stuart v. Laird* to induce the Supreme Court under Chief Justice Marshall to continue pursuing a partisan agenda. The importance of the two cases lay precisely in the possibility that the Marshall Court might have continued the earlier partisan policies of the Federalist judiciary. But with Marshall refusing to assume a partisan posture, consensus developed, as the Republicans under Jefferson had to approve of the way the Court decided the two cases and the Federalists found themselves unable to dispute the position of the highest-ranking leaders of their party remaining in office after the defeat of President Adams in the 1800 election.

This consensus proved reassuring for most Americans after the frightful partisanship of the 1800 election and the immediately preceding years. Permanently organized political parties, as we now know them, had never been part of British or colonial political ideology during the eighteenth century, and they remained foreign to American political thinking as the nineteenth century began. Leaders of government, it was thought, should act in the interests and for the benefit of the entire citizenry, not just on behalf of those who had voted in their favor. Opposition to such disinterested leaders appeared equally inappropriate; as long as the leaders of the community were acting on behalf of all its citizens, those who opposed them had to be acting on behalf only of a few. Of course, parties and factions frequently surfaced, but they were the subjects of condemnation not merely because of particular policies they favored but because of their very existence.

One reason Americans distrusted political factions was a fear that they would propel society into chaos and civil strife. Many Americans living in the aftermath of the election of 1800 could remember a time a quarter-century earlier when political conflict had dissolved into war. Although that war had come to a glorious conclusion with Great Britain's recognition of American independence, the experience nonetheless had involved pain: loved ones had died, neighbors had gone into exile, and property had been destroyed.

There were some signs in 1800 that factional politics could again descend into civil strife. The uprising of farmers in western Massachusetts known as Shays' Rebellion was little more than a decade old, and, as recently as 1795, President Washington had found it necessary to lead a contingent of armed men to put down the Whiskey Rebellion in Pennsylvania, which arose out of a refusal to pay federal excise taxes on liquor. The coercive power of the national government also had been used in 1798 against Jeffersonian editors who had attacked the policies of the Adams administration, and, partly in response to the jailing of the editors, the legislatures of Kentucky and Virginia had hinted at possible use of some vague power to nullify allegedly unconstitutional federal legislation. No one yet knew that major civil strife in America lay a distant six decades in the future, and that in the interval lay the Era of Good Feelings, when political parties would largely disappear, and the Age of Jackson, when political parties finally would be institutionalized.

Thus, when *Marbury v. Madison* used the doctrine of judicial review to curb partisan excesses and move the nation back toward its eighteenth-century tradition of consensus government, most Americans felt relieved. Almost no one objected to the case's ringing endorsement of judicial review and the rule of law. Later generations would find judicial review controversial, but Americans at the time of *Marbury* did not.

Although there had been some controversy about the doctrine during the 1780s, that controversy had dissipated by the opening decade of the nineteenth century. The legitimacy of judicial review is best shown, perhaps, by its general acceptance in early nineteenth-century state courts. By 1820, it appears, eleven of the original thirteen states were publishing reports of their cases, and the courts of ten of them had either invalidated acts of their legislatures or unequivocally asserted their right to do so. Moreover, all five of the states admitted to the Union between 1790 and 1815 had accepted judicial review by 1820, while the four states admitted between 1815 and 1819 all accepted the doctrine in cases published in the first two volumes of their reports. By 1820, in short, the principle of judicial review was, according to the 1817 Pennsylvania case of *Moore v. Houston*, "well established by the great mass of opinion, at the bar, on the bench and in the legislative assemblies of the United States."

Judicial review was so uncontroversial during the early nineteenth century in part because judges and lawyers, as they adopted the doctrine, articulated a rationale for it that was consistent with basic American political assumptions and also because courts in the first two decades of the century did not use the doctrine, as they do today, to determine conflicting issues of social policy.

The rationale for judicial review rested upon the unique American conception of sovereignty that had developed during and after the founding-era debates. Americans had then rejected the traditional British view that the legislature possessed complete sovereignty, and many had begun to argue instead that sovereignty lay with the people, who by a constitution delegated limited power to the legislature.

Legislators, according to the 1793 Virginia case of *Kamper v. Hawkins*, were mere "servants of the people," and a constitution, according to *Cohen v. Hoff*, an 1814 South Carolina case, "the commission from whence [they] . . . derive[d] their power." It "follow[ed]," said the Ohio Supreme Court in 1807 in *Rutherford v. M'Faddon*, "that any act in violation of the constitution, or infringing its provisions must be void, because the legislature, when they step beyond the bounds assigned them, act without authority, and their doings are no more than the doings of any other private man." The judiciary, whose duty, according to *Kamper v. Hawkins*, was "to expound *what the law is*," simply "compare[d] the legislative *act*," said *Rutherford v. M'Faddon*, "with the *constitution*." Since the Constitution clearly "[could not] be adjudged void," the *Rutherford* court added that judges had no choice but to declare any "*act* which . . . [was] inconsistent with it . . . [to] be *no law*." For judges to do otherwise would be to violate their oaths and to join with the legislature in violating the Constitution. Thus, judicial declarations of unconstitutionality were unavoidable and did not, according to *Federalist No. 78*, "suppose a superiority of the judicial to the legislative power," but only, as stated in an early nineteenth-century treatise on the Constitution, "that the power of the people is superior to both."

The doctrine of judicial review, *Kamper v. Hawkins* declared, was not thought to authorize courts to "determine upon the equity, necessity, or usefulness of a law." No one doubted that courts should ignore considerations about the wisdom or expediency of a law when passing upon its validity; to weigh them, *Kamper* added, "would amount to an express interfering with the legislative branch."

Everyone agreed with Georgia's 1808 decision in *Grimball v. Ross* that courts should decide constitutional cases on the basis of "fixed principles . . . stamped with the seals of truth and authority." Their agreement was merely a corollary of an established tenet elaborated in Blackstone's *Commentaries* that judges ought not to "pronounce a new law, but to maintain and expound the old one," and, although that tenet was slowly breaking down in the early nineteenth century, people remained convinced until the 1820s that judges could draw a line between what a federal district judge in *United States v. The William* in 1808 labeled "legal discretion" and "political discretion"— between what *Federalist No. 78* called the exercise of "*judgment*" and the "exercise [of] *will*," and between "declaring," in the language of an 1808 Virginia case, "what the law is, and . . . making a new law." Judicial review, as it developed after the 1780s, was thought, in sum, only to give the people—a single, cohesive, and indivisible body politic—protection against faithless legislators who betrayed the trust placed in them, and not to give judges authority to make law by resolving disputes between interest groups into which the people and their legislative representatives were divided.

For several decades after 1800, judges were able in cases involving judicial review to leave to legislatures the resolution of social conflicts among politically organized or identifiable interest groups and to decide only narrow questions of an apparent legal nature. During those decades, judges were rarely called upon to resolve policy conflicts. Many judicial review cases, for example, were of immediate concern only to the rather small number of individuals directly involved; they decided no more than the constitutionality either of private acts granting new trials in pending litigation or of such trivial or parochial matters as the right of a sheriff to plead his recapture of an escaped debtor as a defense to a suit by a creditor, the power of the City of Philadelphia to enact a building code, and the liability of delinquent clerks to certain statutory penalties.

Other cases, like *Marbury*, while arising out of politically divisive circumstances, could be disposed of on grounds that were not divisive. A New Jersey case refusing to permit a US senator simultaneously to hold the office of county clerk is a prime example: it raised an issue concerning which of two political factions would control an important local office, but the court was able to avoid that issue and deduce its holding from widely accepted principles of republican government that frowned upon plural office holding. As a result, the case did not permanently favor one faction over the other or involve the judiciary in the decision of fundamental social issues underlying the factional split: it left the factions free to contest those issues in the legislative and electoral forums.

Stuart v. Laird was an example of another large category of cases. These cases, in which courts again refused to overrule legislative policy judgments, involved judicial review of statutes altering the composition, jurisdiction, or procedure of the courts. The statutes at issue typically had been passed after a campaign by radical reformers during the three decades after the Revolution to substitute popular for professional control of the legal system. Nevertheless, the statutes in large part reflected a rejection of the radical demands and a conscious policy decision by legislatures not to change the legal system fundamentally. When their constitutionality was later challenged in the courts, there was no opportunity for reconsideration of this policy decision. All the courts could do was affirm it, for their only options were either to invalidate the statutes and thereby preserve the legal system without any change or to uphold them and thereby acquiesce in the legislature's policy of minor but not fundamental change.

There were, of course, some cases in which the courts could have overturned legislation resolving divisive social conflicts between competing political interest groups. But the key fact is that, between about 1790 and 1820, the judiciary did not invalidate such legislation. The relation of church and state, for example, was a prime cause of political division in Massachusetts and Virginia in the decades near the turn of the century. In both states, legislatures after a decade of debate took steps in the direction of disestablishment; in both, the courts accepted legislative policy judgments and upheld the constitutionality of the disestablishing acts.

Another social conflict that produced political divisions in many states arose from squatters placing improvements upon land they were wrongfully occupying; when the Tennessee legislature adopted an act giving squatters the right to recover the value of their improvements if the true owners sued successfully to recover the land, the Tennessee courts again accepted the legislature's resolution of the conflict and upheld the act's constitutionality. State courts also upheld other potentially sensitive legislation, such as a Georgia act postponing debt collection suits and a Pennsylvania act for regulation of the militia. And on the federal level, where the government's conduct of foreign relations had provided the chief impetus to the creation of party divisions, the lower federal courts again sustained a significant legislative decision—the Embargo Act of 1807.

The one subject on which courts invalidated significant legislation involved what we have come to know as takings cases—that is, cases in which legislators sought either to take alleged property rights from original owners and grant them to others or to limit the original owners' use rights. Chief Justice Marshall, it will be recalled, had treated *Marbury* itself as a sort of takings case: in Marshall's view a commission for office was analogous to a patent for land, and thus he regarded Madison's refusal to deliver Marbury's commission as analogous to a legislature's seizure of someone's land. If Marshall had not invalidated section 13 of the Judiciary Act and thereby held that the Supreme Court was an inappropriate forum for granting relief to Marbury, he would have protected Marbury's property in his office just as he would have protected anyone else's property in land.

Marshall continued to uphold property rights in subsequent cases. The next case in which he did so was *Fletcher v. Peck*, which involved the validity of two Georgia acts. The first act had granted land to individuals who had proceeded to sell it to others, who purchased it without notice of possible defects in the title and then subsequently passed their title to the plaintiff, Fletcher; the second act had repealed the first act on the ground that the first had been enacted because several state legislators had been bribed. The Court was asked to invalidate the first act because of the bribery, but Marshall declined to do so because "the principle by which judicial interference would be regulated . . . [could] not [be] clearly discerned." The validity of the first act was not properly a legal question because the Court could find no fixed, uncontroversial standards by which to resolve it.

On the other hand, Marshall readily voided the second act, because it violated "certain great principles of justice, whose authority is universally acknowledged." The issue in *Fletcher v. Peck* was, he observed, "in its nature a question of title"—more specifically, a question of legislative power to revoke a grant of land by claiming that the grant had been fraudulently obtained. According to Marshall, the law of land title was clear: "If a suit be brought to set aside a conveyance obtained by fraud, and the fraud be clearly proved, the conveyance will be set aside, as between the parties; but the rights of third persons, who are purchasers without notice, for a valuable consideration, cannot be disregarded." For the Georgia legislature to feel "itself absolved from those rules of property which are common to all the citizens of the United States, and from those principles of equity which are acknowledged in all our courts" was for it to act on the authority of "its power alone." The same power could be used to "divest any other individual of his lands, if it shall be the will of the legislature to exert it."

In sum, the Court had to invalidate one of two Georgia statutes in *Fletcher v. Peck*. It did not, however, undertake what Marshall saw as the essentially political task of identifying which of a legislator's motives for supporting a bill were legitimate. Rather, it appealed to what seemed a fixed legal principle incorporated in the contract clause of the Constitution and relied upon by the vast majority of American people: that a legislature could not take back land that it had granted away.

The most famous of the takings cases—the *Dartmouth College Case*—was a variation on the same theme. It grew out of a political controversy that had roused statewide attention, but that controversy involved mere questions of patronage and personality unrelated to the legal issues on which the parties argued and the courts disposed of the case.

The dispute arose when the New Hampshire legislature attempted to revoke not a grant of land but a grant of corporate governing privileges that had been made to self-perpetuating trustees who had received land and money from other individuals. It came to the Supreme Court after a lengthy, bitter political controversy in the state. The Court voided the repeal act because it constituted a taking of vested rights protected by the contract clause. Again Marshall appealed to shared general principles to support his holding, noting that "the parties in this case differ less on general principles . . . than on the application of those principles to this case." The parties agreed that "if the act of incorporation be a grant of political power . . . or if the State of New Hampshire, as a government, be alone interested in its transactions, the subject [was] one in which the legislature of the State may act according to its own judgment. . . . But if this be a private eleemosynary institution, endowed with a capacity to take property for objects unconnected with government, whose funds are bestowed by individuals on the faith of the charter," then the legislature was restrained by the "limitation of its power imposed by the constitution of the United States." After painstakingly analyzing the facts, Marshall found Dartmouth College a private institution whose property the state accordingly could not take. This disposition of *Dartmouth College*, like the Court's disposition of *Fletcher v. Peck*, aroused little criticism from contemporaries.

Takings cases in state courts were similarly decided. For example, in the 1807 Massachusetts case of *Ellis v. Marshall*, Justice Isaac Parker, deciding the constitutionality of an act that taxed an individual for the construction of a road, distinguished between "public act[s], predicated upon a view to the general good," and "private act[s], obtained at the solicitation of individuals, for their private emolument, or for the improvement of their estates." Although he concluded that courts could not interfere with legislative evaluations of the general good, Parker invalidated the tax act because it subjected an individual "to taxation, *volens nolens* [against his or her will], for the promotion of a private enterprize." Similarly, in the 1816 New York case of *Gardner v. Village of Newburgh*, Chancellor Kent voided not a tax but an uncompensated diversion of Gardner's stream by the village. Without compensation, such a taking of private property for public use was "unjust, and contrary to the first principles of government," principles "admitted by the soundest authorities, and . . . adopted by all temperate and civilized governments."

When early nineteenth-century judges refrained from deciding highly controversial questions and merely protected vested property rights that few Americans questioned, they were not subjected to political attacks. Since most white, male Americans owned land already or expected to acquire land at some point during their lives, they did not want to see government use its takings power to challenge land titles. No organized or identifiable groups or parties had yet formed to urge use of eminent domain for redistributive purposes, and thus, when judges struck down statutes that took land without providing compensation, their decisions seemed nonpolitical. In short, the issue decided in the takings cases—the scope of state power to seize private property—was not yet a politically divisive one, but one for which judges could find answers by reference to broadly shared beliefs about the nature of republican government.

Thus, as one surveys the cases between about 1790 and 1820 involving claims that state statutes violated state constitutions or that federal statutes violated the federal Constitution, a persistent pattern emerges. The pattern discloses that the courts by 1820 had begun to hold legislation unconstitutional with some frequency, but that their working understanding of the scope of their constitutional activity was sufficiently different from ours that, although we term their activity judicial review, we must not lose sight of the difference.

Early nineteenth-century courts, unlike our own, still sought to leave, and in fact succeeded in leaving, to legislatures the resolution of conflicts between organized social interest groups. Once a legislature had resolved a conflict in a manner having widespread public support, judges would in practice view the resolution as that of the people at large, even though one or more organized groups continued to oppose it, and would give it conclusive effect, at least as long as a finding of inconsistency with the constitution was not plain and unavoidable. Judges of the early nineteenth century such as John Marshall, unlike judges of today, did not see judicial review as a mechanism for protecting minority rights against majoritarian infringement.

Early judicial review thus rested upon a perception of political reality that differed sharply from current perceptions. Judges of the early nineteenth century viewed "the people" as a politically homogeneous and cohesive body possessing common political goals and aspirations, not as a congeries of factions and interest groups, each having its own set of goals and aspirations. The concern of judges in early constitutional cases was with the potentiality of conflict between legislators and their constituents—with the possibility that faithless legislators might betray the trust placed in them by the people. The perceived purpose of judicial review was to protect the people from such possible betrayals, not to impose obstacles in the path of decisions made by the people's agents in due execution of their trust. As a result, little popular objection arose either to the doctrine of judicial review or to the leading Supreme Court case, *Marbury v. Madison*, that had proclaimed it.

But the political consensus underlying the early nineteenth-century practice of judicial review could not endure. As the circle of politically active Americans expanded during the course of the century, constitutional principles, especially principles about the sanctity of private property, became the subject of political debate. As a result, some new foundation for judicial review was needed. In the next chapter we shall examine how, at the very time judicial review was becoming established as a fixture of the American constitutional system, its Marshallian foundations were eroded. Then we shall turn in future chapters to the process in the twentieth century by which new foundations for the practice were articulated, both in America and ultimately around the world.

CHAPTER TEN

Judicial Review Becomes Politically Charged

Neither the doctrine of judicial review nor the cases decided pursuant to the doctrine aroused significant controversy during the three decades from 1790 to 1820, in the midst of which *Marbury v. Madison* was decided. Like Chief Justice Marshall, many judges avoided conflict with legislatures over controversial issues of political or social import. Statutes that were declared unconstitutional, like the section of the Judiciary Act of 1789 invalidated in the *Marbury* case, typically involved narrow issues of judicial jurisdiction and procedure of little interest to any larger political public. Even cases passing upon the power of legislatures to seize and regulate property aroused little controversy since nearly all politically active Americans owned property and applauded judicial attempts to protect private rights from legislative infringement.

Judicial review also was noncontroversial in the early nineteenth century because courts exercised the function only on rare occasions. After declaring section 13 of the 1789 Judiciary Act unconstitutional in *Marbury v. Madison*, the Supreme Court did not invalidate another act of Congress for fifty-four years. State courts similarly were far less active in striking down state legislation in the early part of the nineteenth century than they would be in the later part.

Like the Supreme Court of the United States, the Supreme Court of Indiana held only two legislative acts unconstitutional prior to 1850, while the Supreme Judicial Court of Massachusetts struck down only ten state statutes before 1860. The highest Court of Virginia invalidated only four laws prior to 1860. Courts were most active in judicial review cases in New York, but even there few statutes were invalidated prior to 1850, at least in comparison with the number declared unconstitutional after 1850; only ten statutes were held void prior to 1840, and only eighteen were invalidated between 1841 and 1850.

There was only one case in the first half of the nineteenth century—*Eakin v. Raub*—in which controversy over the doctrine of judicial review materialized. In *Eakin*, Pennsylvania's Judge John Banister Gibson authored a dissenting opinion advocating abandonment of judicial review. Gibson recited all the common arguments against the doctrine. He noted that "repugnance to the constitution is not always self-evident" and that, since people "seldom . . . think exactly alike," "conflicts" in interpreting constitutional provisions would be "inevitable." If the judiciary once entered into considerations of unconstitutionality, he wondered, "where shall it stop."

For Gibson, in short, there were no clear lines, particularly since review of the constitutionality of legislation required judges to make what he labeled "political" as distinguished from "civil" or legal determinations. He further argued that the legislature possessed "pre-eminence" in government; "the power of the legislature," according to Gibson, is "the power of the people, and sovereign as far as it extends." Gibson simply could see no basis for courts to question political decisions made by the people; for him, judicial review denied "a *postulate* in the theory of our government, and the very basis of the superstructure, that the people are wise, virtuous, and competent to manage their own affairs."

Ultimately, though, in the 1830s, 1840s, and 1850s, Gibson's views were rejected, and judges in their opinions began to articulate new justifications for judicial review. One justification was the weight of precedent: by 1860 courts had held legislation unconstitutional in over 150 cases. As one North Carolina judge observed in 1861 in the case of *Barnes v. Barnes*, "the right, and the duty of this Court, to give judgment on the constitutional power of the Legislature in making statutes, . . . [has been] established by so many elaborated opinions of this Court, and of the Supreme Court of the United States, and of our sister States, as to make a further discussion or citation of authorities a useless attempt at a display of learning." Courts, according to the 1848 Georgia case of *Flint River Steamboat Co. v. Foster*, would "not stop, at [that] late day, to inquire" into "their duty to declare Acts of the Legislature, repugnant to the Constitution, void," for while "these grave questions once elicited much discussion," the matter now seemed settled; as the New York Court of Appeals declared in the leading 1856 case of *Wynehamer v. People*, "the right of courts to

declare legislative enactments, in derogation of the constitution, void
. . . [had] been too long and steadily exercised in this country to be
now doubted or questioned."

Indeed, even Judge Gibson felt compelled by 1845 to recant his
former views, in part because of the weight of authority favoring
judicial review and the apparent acquiescence of the people therein.
In the 1845 case of *Norris v. Clymer*, Gibson announced that he now
had come to favor judicial review "from experience of the necessity
of the case." "Experience [had] prove[d]" to Gibson that the constitution was "thoughtlessly but habitually violated." Other judges
agreed. In *De Chastellux v. Fairchild*, the Pennsylvania Supreme
Court observed again in 1850 that "great wrongs may undoubtedly
be perpetrated by legislative bodies," which "from mistaken views of
policy," in the language of the Michigan case of *People v. Gallagher*
some six years later, often passed legislation "greatly injurious to
the best interests of the State, or . . . oppressive in its operation on
one class of citizens." One New York trial judge in an 1848 case, for
example, thought "*excessive legislation* . . . [to be] the great legal curse
of the age . . . drawing every thing within its grasp," while California
and Indiana judges, in *People ex rel. Attorney General v. Burbank* in
1859 and in *Beebe v. State* in 1855 respectively, found their "statute
book[s] . . . replete with crude and unconstitutional legislation" and
other "very odious enactment[s]."

By the middle of the nineteenth century, in short, judicial review
had become an accepted feature of American law. The public had
acquiesced in it, and no one doubted that judges had jurisdiction to
declare legislative acts unconstitutional and void. Indeed, the doctrine of judicial review had become so firmly established that no one
could any longer question its propriety. With the doctrine firmly established, judges began to exercise their power of review with greater
frequency, and they also began to use the power in a fashion that
involved them in substantial controversy.

A marked change occurred in the frequency of cases invalidating
legislation. Although the US Supreme Court had declared only two
acts of Congress void prior to 1860, it held twenty-one unconstitutional between 1865 and 1898. Similarly, the number of instances in
which state courts held state legislation unconstitutional rose to 31
between 1860 and 1893 in Massachusetts, to 40 between 1861 and

1902 in Virginia, to 94 between 1850 and 1899 in Indiana, and to 266 between 1851 and 1900 in New York. The Ohio Supreme Court was also very active in the 1880s and 1890s, as it struck down 57 legislative acts, while in Minnesota, approximately 70 statutes were held void between 1885 and 1899.

Not only did growth occur in the number of instances of judicial review; the second half of the nineteenth century also witnessed an increase in the controversial nature of many of the issues on which judges passed. The trend began in the late 1850s with two cases in leading courts—the Supreme Court of the United States and the Court of Appeals of New York. The two cases were *Scott v. Sandford* and *Wynehamer v. People*, in both of which the courts acted, as their predecessors had earlier in the century, to protect private property rights. But in both cases, protection of property clashed with powerful reform movements—namely, antislavery and temperance—and as a result, the judiciary's protection of property rights was not received with the same equanimity as the public in earlier decades had received it.

The *Dred Scott* case, which was decided in 1857, involved two issues. The first was whether the federal court in which Scott had commenced his case had jurisdiction. Scott's claim of jurisdiction was predicated upon diversity of citizenship: Scott claimed to be a citizen of Missouri, while the defendant, John Sandford, was a citizen of New York. Sandford responded, however, and the Supreme Court ruled that African Americans could not be citizens and hence could not maintain suits such as the one brought by Dred Scott in federal courts. This jurisdictional finding would have been an adequate basis for dismissing Scott's claim and declining to pass on its merits, but the Court did not rest its holding on lack of jurisdiction alone and proceeded to the second issue raised by Scott—his claim of freedom.

Scott had based his claim, at least in part, on the fact that a previous master had taken him to reside at Fort Snelling, then in the Territory of Upper Louisiana and now in Minnesota, which Congress in the Missouri Compromise of 1820 had declared to be free territory. The Supreme Court answered this claim by declaring the Missouri Compromise unconstitutional. Rejecting the argument that the provision in the Northwest Ordinance of 1787 prohibiting slavery provided a precedent for congressional prohibition of slavery in other territories, the Court held that Congress had a constitutional obligation to keep all territories open for settlement and development by citizens of all states, including slave owners, and that fulfillment of that obligation necessitated protection of the property of citizens, including their property in slaves.

This decision infuriated antislavery proponents. Although it was no longer possible to claim that the Supreme Court lacked authority to declare acts of Congress unconstitutional, antislavery leaders frequently maintained that the Court's holding would not bar Congress from enacting and enforcing future antislavery legislation, subject to review by future Supreme Courts. Moreover, they argued that the Court had erred in declaring the Missouri Compromise unconstitutional. According to an 1857 report to the New York legislature, the invalidation of the Missouri Compromise was "contrary to the fundamental principle . . . that every man has an inalienable right to his liberty, and that it can only be taken from him by a statute of the State in which he lives." Liberty, according to the advocates of antislavery, was the natural state of people, whereas slavery—that is, property in people—could occur only when local police regulations altered that natural state. For the forces of antislavery that would soon capture control of Congress and the presidency in the 1860 elections, the Supreme Court got it backward when it protected property rather than liberty from legislative regulation and encroachment.

A year earlier, in 1856, the Court of Appeals of New York had decided another controversial case, *Wynehamer v. People*. *Wynehamer* reflected a clash between property rights and temperance advocates who were striving to purify society by forbidding consumption of alcoholic beverages. The narrow issue presented to the court was whether state legislation prohibiting the sale of alcoholic beverages could be applied to liquors owned by individuals before passage of the act; the court of appeals concluded that the owners had a vested property right and that legislation interfering with that right was therefore unconstitutional.

As had been true in the aftermath of *Dred Scott*, little question arose concerning the power of judicial review; the controversy was about the substantive issue in the case—whether to protect alleged private rights of property or to promote the perfectionist scheme of temperance advocates. Whatever decision it reached, the court would disappoint a powerful political group; as one judge wrote, that "danger" arose "when[ever] theories, alleged to be founded in natural reason or inalienable rights, but subversive of the just and necessary powers of government, attract[ed] the belief of considerable classes of men."

In the last third of the nineteenth century, judges continued to confront cases in which claims of property rights and individual economic liberty stood in opposition to reform programs of powerful political groups. In the US Supreme Court, the two most important cases were *Munn v. Illinois* and *Pollock v. Farmers' Loan & Trust Co.*

In *Munn*, the Court upheld the Granger laws that had been enacted by the Illinois legislature at the behest of farmers and their political allies for the purpose of regulating railroads and grain dealers. The specific statute at issue regulated the prices charged by warehouses in the city of Chicago, the owners of which claimed that, as holders of private property, they were immune from legislative regulation. The Supreme Court did not question the starting proposition that private property owners were exempt from regulation, but it did hold that, since the warehouses were affected with a public interest, the claim of their owners to immunity was lost. *Munn* was like *Marbury*, in that the Court avoided a direct, head-on conflict with a powerful legislative majority, but it also was unlike *Marbury*, in that it involved a major social controversy pitting a majoritarian legislature against private individuals seeking to resist legislative power.

Pollock v. Farmers' Loan & Trust Co. again pitted a majoritarian legislature—in this instance, the Congress of the United States—against private wealth holders. In *Pollock*, the Supreme Court not only failed to avoid, but indeed exacerbated the confrontation by declaring the federal income tax unconstitutional, in part on the ground that its progressive rate structure resulted in unequal taxation. The crisis generated by *Pollock* was resolved only when Congress proposed and three-fourths of the states ratified what is arguably the most significant provision of the Constitution—the Sixteenth Amendment, which made the constitutionality of a progressive income tax unquestionable.

Analogous cases pitting property and other individual economic rights against legislative regulatory power occurred during the closing decades of the nineteenth century in the state courts. Arising out of the same social conflict as *Wynehamer v. People* was *McCullough v. Brown*, where the Supreme Court of South Carolina declared unconstitutional an act that gave the state a monopoly of the liquor trade; the court thought the state monopoly would interfere with the liberty of individuals to enter the trade for themselves.

Other state cases saw legislative efforts to improve working conditions of laborers founder on the rocks of economic liberty. Thus, in New York, the 1885 case of *Matter of Jacobs* struck down legislation prohibiting the manufacture of cigars in tenement houses unless certain health and safety regulations were satisfied. In Pennsylvania, *Godcharles v. Wigeman*, decided in 1886, invalidated an act requiring mining and manufacturing companies to pay wages only in currency, while an 1893 case, *State v. Loomis*, held the similar Missouri "scrip" act unconstitutional. Analogous legislation, requiring corporations to pay wages on a weekly basis, was invalidated by the Illinois Supreme Court in 1893 in *Braceville Coal Co. v. People*.

In deciding in these cases to protect property rights and individual economic liberty at the expense of those who were using legislative power to promote their vision of a just and good society, judges were seen by progressive reformers to be engaging in a fundamentally different activity than that in which John Marshall had engaged when his Court, early in the nineteenth century, had commenced the judiciary's protection of property. Marshall had restricted judicial review mainly to cases in which statutes could be invalidated on the basis of a widely shared consensus about the limitations of legislative power. He had conceptualized judicial review as a mechanism for protecting the public at large against faithless legislators. Aware that they lacked power to coerce acceptance of their judgments, Marshall and his contemporaries on the bench rarely attempted to impose the views of one segment of society upon another. Theirs was a quaint conception of judicial review, quite unlike the conception with which we today are familiar.

By the latter part of the nineteenth century, however, judicial review had begun to take on a more modern look. It was beginning to be seen not as a device for protecting the people against their government, but as a protection for minorities against majorities.

Long before the mid-nineteenth century, it was axiomatic, in the words of one delegate to the 1821 New York constitutional convention, that the function of politics was "to secure to the majority of the people that control and influence in every section of the state to which they are justly entitled." Yet political majoritarianism raised difficulties. Courts well knew, as stated in the 1850 Pennsylvania case of *De Chastellux v. Fairchild*, that legislatures concerned only with the interests of the majority would willingly sanction "the sacrifice of individual right" since individual rights were "too remotely connected with the objects and contests of the masses to attract their attention." Minorities, that is, could not protect themselves in the legislative process. As another Pennsylvania judge explained in 1851 in *Ervine's Appeal*:

> When, in the exercise of proper legislative powers, general laws are enacted, which bear or may bear on the whole community, if they are unjust and against the spirit of the constitution, the whole community will be interested to procure their repeal by a voice potential. And that is the great security for just and fair legislation.
>
> But when individuals are selected from the mass, and laws are enacted affecting their property, without summons or notice, at the instigation of an interested party, who is to stand up for them, thus isolated from the mass, in injury and injustice, or where are they to seek relief from such acts of despotic power?

The judge answered his question by granting to minorities a "refuge . . . in the courts, the only secure place for determining conflicting rights by due course of law." Without such refuge, the Michigan Supreme Court declared in 1856 in *People v. Gallagher*, minorities would "stand in no better attitude, irrespective of the fundamental principles and maxims of free government, than that of the most abject slaves to the majority." Indeed, the Ohio Supreme Court expressed its fear in the 1851 case of *Griffith v. Commissioners* that "if the rights of *minorities* . . . [were] not observed, it . . . [would] not be long before the *majorities* . . . [themselves would] be in bondage."

Thus, by the 1850s, the courts had articulated a new theoretical justification for judicial review: that it was needed, according to an 1831 Tennessee case, "to secure to weak and unpopular minorities and individuals, equal rights with the majority"; according to an 1836 case, also in Tennessee, "to prevent majorities in times of high political excitement from passing partial laws"; and, according to an 1851 New York case, to protect "minorities against the caprices, recklessness, or prejudices of majorities." Or, as one Virginia judge had summarized the theory in *Goddin v. Crump* as early as 1837:

> It must be admitted that at the institution of civil government founded on the rights of all, the will of the majority must prevail over the opinions and interests of the minority: but when such government is established, its great object is to protect the rights of the minority from the tyranny of the majority; a tyranny more inflexible and implacable than the tyranny of a single despot. . . . To effect this relief against the tyranny of majorities, written constitutions were devised by the American people.

By the middle of the nineteenth century, in short, judicial review had become reestablished on a new basis—the basis on which it would function in *Scott v. Sandford* and *Pollock v. Farmers' Loan & Trust Co.* and in numerous twentieth-century cases. No longer a device for protecting the people as a whole from faithless legislators, judicial review had become a means for sectional and political minorities or individuals lacking control of the legislative process to obtain reconsideration of the legislature's decisions and overturn the legislature's political judgments. It had become a vehicle through which judges could keep the nation loyal to what they thought were the fundamental precepts of American life. Contrary to its original conception, judicial review, as the Indiana Supreme Court proclaimed in *Beebe v. State* in 1851, had become a mechanism for the courts "to protect the people against themselves."

But judicial review in the late nineteenth century still had not assumed what would become its late twentieth and early twenty-first century form. Judicial review had not yet come to protect the interests of powerless minorities identified on racial, ethnic, religious, or sexual grounds. On the contrary, its purpose, according to Christopher Tiedeman's 1886 *Treatise on the Limitations of the Police Power*, was to protect the most powerful of minorities—the rich—against "governmental interference," which was demanded everywhere as a sufficient panacea for every social evil which threatens the prosperity of society. Socialism, Communism, and Anarchism are rampant throughout the civilized world. The State is called on to protect the weak against the shrewdness of the stronger, to determine what wages a workman shall receive for his labor, and how many hours daily he shall labor.

Contemplating these extraordinary demands of the great army of discontents, and their apparent power, with the growth and development of universal suffrage, to enforce their views of civil polity upon the civilized world, the conservative classes stand in constant fear of the advent of an absolutism more tyrannial and more unreasoning than any before experienced by man, the absolutism of a democratic majority.

In short, judicial review had emerged, Tiedeman continued, as the means "to protect private rights against the radical experimentation of social reformers . . . in the cause of social order." From the perspective of progressive reformers and historians who, in the early decades of the twentieth century, would author the first histories of judicial review, protecting private property against regulatory legislation involved policy choice and judicial intrusion into the domain of politics. For reasons about to be examined, however, conservative lawyers and their judicial supporters could still understand themselves to be acting in a legal capacity in property rights cases.

CHAPTER ELEVEN

The Judiciary as Protector of Minorities

The crux of the original decision in *Marbury v. Madison*, as we have seen, was John Marshall's distinction between law and politics. Law dealt with those matters as to which there existed substantial community acquiescence in fixed, unchanging rules. In response to those rules juries could render unanimous verdicts and courts generally could expect compliance with their mandates. Politics, in contrast, involved questions about which the nation, the states, and local communities were divided. In connection with those questions, judges could not expect randomly chosen juries routinely to reach unanimous verdicts, nor could judges themselves have a basis for deciding to accept the views of one political faction rather than the views of another. All courts could do was place their trust in the majoritarian electoral process and defer to the decisions of elected legislatures and executive officials.

For more than a century after the *Marbury* case was handed down, conservative jurists were able largely to maintain Marshall's distinction between law and politics and to understand that they were enforcing legal rights rather than making political decisions when they held acts of the coordinate, legislative branch unconstitutional. Thus, we have seen how at the time of *Marbury* and for several decades thereafter, judges routinely refrained from entering the political thicket and applied the doctrine of judicial review mainly to issues of narrow scope that aroused little political interest or controversy. Usually, courts were able to apply the doctrine of judicial review only to statutes that legislators had passed in betrayal of the trust reposed by their constituents and thereby to appear to be upholding the will of the people against their faithless agents.

On occasion, of course, judges trespassed upon the political domain, as in the 1857 Supreme Court decision of *Scott v. Sandford*, which declared the Missouri Compromise of 1820 unconstitutional and held that slave owners could maintain their property in slaves in any territory of the United States. On those occasions, political leaders who disagreed with the courts' results criticized their decisions, campaigned against them, and ultimately ignored them. In the aftermath of the *Dred Scott* case, for example, leaders of the Republican Party turned the Supreme Court's holding into a contentious issue in the 1858 and 1860 elections and when they gained majorities in Congress in 1861, promptly enacted and enforced legislation prohibiting slavery in the territories, despite the fact that the Court in *Dred Scott* had declared such laws unconstitutional.

When courts in the *Marbury* era initially began striking down legislative infringements of private property rights, they were again acting in support of a legal consensus on which the public as a whole agreed. Even when, in the late nineteenth century, the scope of legislative power over private property became a more contentious issue, judges could still understand that they were enforcing legal rights against legislative power. They could understand, in the closing decades of the century, that they had been protecting property from legislative infringement for several decades, and in many cases they merely had to follow precedent in order to continue providing protection. Moreover, although the distribution of wealth was becoming increasingly unequal, most voters still owned or expected to own property and therefore remained committed to a legal regime of private property rights. Thus, late nineteenth and early twentieth-century judges could and often did invalidate legislation affecting private property on the ground that such legislation responded to the demands of special interests and violated long-standing, fundamental norms of the American polity.

The notion that judicial review merely protected legal rights rather than adjudicating political controversies collapsed, however, in the late 1930s. Beginning in those years, the line between law and politics grew increasingly blurred, as judges began to trespass more and more frequently upon domains they had previously left to the democratic political process. The underlying cause was a growing loss of faith in that process.

By the 1930s, popular government and the institutions of mass democracy had become problematic. Manipulations of mass politics in that and recent decades had put Hitler and Mussolini into power in Germany and Italy, transformed Senator Huey Long and Father Charles Coughlin into national figures famed for their opposition to President Franklin D. Roosevelt's New Deal, and led to mass oppression of minorities in Germany and the American South. As what the chaplain of Columbia University labeled the "shadow of the swastika" spread across Europe in the final years of the 1930s, American thinkers like the chaplain Dr. Raymond C. Knox, grew concerned about the "menace to . . . freedom" that it posed and urged "all creeds to unite against" what Congressman Vito Marcantonio in 1938 called "that canker of fascism and Nazism" in order to preserve what John Maynard Keynes had earlier called "liberty of thought and criticism." "The rise of totalitarianism," according to the renowned theologian Reinhold Niebuhr, prompted Americans in the closing years of the 1930s "to view all collectivist answers . . . with increased apprehension" and to recognize that "a too powerful state is dangerous to our liberties."

Alarm about the spread of totalitarianism overlapped emerging concerns about interest-group politics—concerns that undercut classical arguments in defense of majoritarian democracy. Supporters of democracy had long argued that if the majority of the people were left free to elect their leaders, the government that resulted would mirror the common will of the people and accordingly would pursue the public good. The realization that the people aligned themselves into interest groups, on the other hand, proved corrosive of the very ideas of common will and public good. In a political culture of interest-group politics, legislation came to appear as favoritism toward some groups at the expense of the freedom and equality of other groups. Judicial review, in turn, no longer appeared as an effort of judges to uphold the law against faithless legislators but as a judicial choice to favor particular interests in the polity against other interests.

Judge Learned Hand was one of the first to elaborate a vision of interest-group politics. In a 1928 speech before the American Law Institute, he observed:

Sometimes . . . we speak of the judges as representing a common-will. . . . [But] they are not charged with power to decide the major conflicts. . . . We think of the legislature as the place for resolving these, and so indeed it is. But if we go further and insist that there at any rate we have an expression of a common-will, . . . we should be wrong again. I will not of course deny that there are statutes of which we can say that they carry something like the assent of a majority. But most legislation is not of that kind; it represents the insistence of a compact and formidable minority.

Two years later a conservative law professor at the University of Pennsylvania, John Dickinson, embellished Hand's earlier insight:

The task of government . . . is not to express an imaginary popular will, but to effect adjustments among the various special wills and purposes which at any given time are pressing for realization. . . . Government, from this point of view, is primarily an arbitrator, and since practically every arbitration must result in giving to one side more of what it thinks it ought to have than the other side is willing to admit, every governmental act can be viewed as favoring in some degree some particular and partial "will," or special interest.

As events unfolded through the 1930s, even New Dealers began to abandon President Roosevelt's early rhetoric, which viewed the masses as "part and parcel of a rounded whole" who understood that "we all go up, or else we all go down, as one people" and "that the welfare of your family or mine cannot be bought at the sacrifice of our neighbor's family." By the late 1930s, at least some New Dealers had learned from experience that the people were divided into special interests. Accordingly they had begun to perceive a need for the enactment of laws designed to promote the organization of economically weak groups so that they might hold their own against stronger rivals.

This development pointed, in turn, toward a redefinition of democracy. As political scientist John Chamberlain wrote in a 1940 book, a democratic "society" was one in which "various groups and classes" whose "power [was] evenly spread," faced each other with "economic checks and balances to parallel the political checks and balances," all of which produced "a state of tension . . . that permit[ted] no one group to dare bid for the total power." Over the next three decades, this view was codified in such classics as V. O. Key's *Politics, Parties, & Pressure Groups*, Douglass Adair's 1951 article rescuing Madison's theory of factions in *Federalist No. 10* from the dustbin of history, and Theodore Lowi's *The End of Liberalism*.

No one better captured the change that occurred in American political ideology as a result of the emergence of interest groups at home and fascism and Nazism abroad than the New Deal senator, Robert F. Wagner. In a 1938 speech, Wagner declared:

> As we reflect sorrowfully on the turn in world events . . . , we pose in our own minds *the essential governmental problem of our times*. In the 18th and 19th centuries, that problem was how to establish the will of the majority in representative government. *In the world of today, the problem is how to protect the integrity and civil liberties of minority races and groups.* The humane solution of that problem is now the supreme test of democratic principles, the test indeed, of civilized government.
>
> We in America have long cherished the picture of a great melting pot. . . . That picture, we must all admit, is marred in this State . . . by certain manifestations of racial intolerance and prejudice. . . . The bestial manifestations of anti-Semitism abroad are happily absent from our national scene. We cannot, however, be blind to the forms of anti-Semitism prevalent at home. These manifestations have been vigorously challenged by spokesmen of all creeds, and many notorious instances have met with effective protest.
>
> Far less effective in marshaling informed public opinion and suffering from discrimination and prejudice so deep-seated as to be taken for granted by the community at large, are the half million Negroes in the State.

After describing graphically the discrimination that victimized African Americans in New York in the 1930s, Wagner concluded, "In the final analysis the so-called Negro problem, or any other minority problem, is but another aspect of man's eternal struggle for freedom and justice, a problem that solves itself when democracy is extended into every phase of our material life."

Few thinkers as early as 1938 had as yet seen the future as clearly as did Wagner in this speech. At that time, many still believed that the essential issue for government was how to establish the will of the majority of the people. For many, however, in the world of today, the issue has become how to end racial, ethnic, and religious intolerance and to protect the integrity and civil liberties of minority races and groups.

Our task is to comprehend the significance for judges and judicial review of this change in the understanding of the essential task of just government. We need to grasp how judicial review changed after the late 1930s. Only then can we fully appreciate how *Marbury v. Madison* was the precursor for, yet distinct from, the judicial review that exists in America and the world today.

In a government charged with the task of effectuating the will of the majority, judicial review has a necessarily small role. As the least democratic branch of government, judges have little basis on which to outguess legislators as to the content of the majority's will. Nor should they attempt to thwart that will. Thus, they can invalidate legislation only to protect the people from the occasionally faithless legislature that has abused its trust or to secure rights that the people in drafting the Constitution had placed outside the jurisdiction of the majoritarian political process.

But if the essential task of just government is to protect the liberty and equality of minorities from an overbearing majority, then undemocratic judges have a special role to play, and their exercise of the power of judicial review of legislation becomes a main instrument of just government. Democratically elected legislators and elected executive officials, who are responsible to popular majorities, cannot be trusted to protect minorities from those majorities. Judges can be.

Supreme Court justice Harlan Fiske Stone came to this realization in the same year that Senator Wagner articulated his new understanding of the essential duty of just government. The timing was not coincidental; both men were responding to the same forces of injustice that they observed spreading in the world. As Stone wrote in a 1938 letter to Judge Irving Lehman of the New York Court of Appeals, he had become "deeply concerned about the increasing racial and religious intolerance which seem[ed] to bedevil the world" and which might "be augmented in this country." For this reason, he had thought it necessary to draft what has since become one of American constitutional law's most important texts—footnote four of *United States v. Carolene Products Co.* The footnote announced that the Court would scrutinize strictly legislation "directed at particular religious, . . . or national, . . . or racial minorities," when "prejudice against discrete and insular minorities may be a special condition, which tends seriously to curtail the operation of those political processes ordinarily to be relied upon to protect minorities." On such occasions, a "correspondingly more searching judicial inquiry" was required to guarantee the fairness, legality, and justice of a majoritarian act.

The Supreme Court's new understanding of the nature and function of judicial review transformed the practice within a few years. In 1938, the same year that Justice Stone wrote *Carolene Products*, the Court decided the first in a line of cases in which it struck down segregation in educational contexts; the line of cases culminated sixteen years later in *Brown v. Board of Education.* Four years after footnote four, the Court handed down its first decision in *Williams v. North Carolina*, which came to the assistance of a then unpopular minority—spouses seeking divorce—and invalidated much state legislative and decisional law placing obstacles in the path of enforcing divorce decrees from jurisdictions other than the state in which a spouse seeking a divorce resided or had married.

The next year, in *West Virginia State Board of Education v. Barnette*, the Court protected the small sect of Jehovah's Witnesses against a popular, majoritarian requirement that they salute the flag—an act deemed sinful pursuant to their religious beliefs. After initial decisions to the contrary, the Court began in the late 1950s to uphold the free speech rights of Communists and other political dissidents. Footnote four of *Carolene Products* arguably came to its fullest fruition in the 1960s and early 1970s, when the Warren Court and its successor, the early Burger Court, reapportioned Congress and the state legislatures, outlawed prayer in public schools, upheld the procedural rights of criminal defendants, and guaranteed many aspects of sexual privacy. The legitimation of same-sex marriage is another step in an analogous direction. In all these cases, the Court came to the defense of unpopular, suspect minorities and invalidated laws with which the vast majority of Americans had agreed.

Of course, the Supreme Court has not always upheld minority rights in the years since 1938. More often than not, it has upheld popular laws adopted through the majoritarian political process despite their negative impact on minorities. And, as the Court vacillated in its judgments about the constitutionality of statutes, sometimes deciding in favor of the interests of minorities and sometimes deciding against them, it routinely made judgments about the desirability of social policies.

The Court has been criticized for making case-by-case policy judgments, and the pull of *Marbury*'s distinction between law and politics has been so strong that the Court has continued to strive earnestly to find legalistic grounds for its decisions independent of the will of political and judicial actors. Justices and students of the Court have argued that the Court should enforce minority rights only if those rights have a basis in the Constitution's text or, alternatively, that in deciding cases, the Court should protect political processes that render government more responsive to genuine majority demands. Others have urged the Court to follow rules of law said to be implicit in the governmental structure established by the Constitution, while still others have urged the Court to derive rules of law from philosophical first principles, whether Kantian or utilitarian. Each of these approaches, it is said, will provide the Supreme Court with fixed legal principles with which to decide cases and will make recourse to ad hoc policy determination unnecessary.

Unfortunately, none of these approaches adequately balances minority rights against majoritarian power. The Founding Fathers did not draft the text of the Constitution with a purpose of securing minority rights as their main goal, nor was the structure of the Constitution designed for that purpose. Kantian and utilitarian philosophy similarly do not have the protection of minorities as their chief ends. Protecting discrete and insular racial, ethnic, and religious minorities is a mid-twentieth-century idea, not an eighteenth- or nineteenth-century one. Of course, decisions, such as those reapportioning legislatures, which are designed to enable majorities among the people to influence legislative decision making more effectively, also will not aid minorities in the protection of their rights.

Ultimately, the critics of the Court are misguided in expecting the justices to decide judicial review cases involving racial, religious, or cultural minorities without making repeated, ad hoc policy judgments. The need for such judgments follows almost ineluctably from the suggestion of Senator Wagner that the essential task of government in our times is not to establish the will of the majority but to protect the integrity and civil liberties of minorities. Legislative majorities are too self-interested to be trusted with that task: some other institution of government is needed. Because of its independence and impartiality, the judiciary appears to be the most promising alternative. But no one has promulgated clear legal principles that can direct judges in the performance of the task. Their job is not to champion the interests of minorities on all occasions, but only when it is fair and just to do so. And in the absence of clear rules, they can only decide what is fair and just by recourse to their intuitions about sound social policy.

CHAPTER TWELVE

The Worldwide Spread of Judicial Review

Until the twentieth century, *Marbury v. Madison* and judicial review of the constitutionality of acts of coordinate legislative bodies were mainly American phenomena. Of course, there were imperial and federal systems in which courts at the central capital determined the validity of legislation that had been adopted at the periphery. The United States itself was such a federal system, in which the Supreme Court routinely decided whether state laws were consistent with federal law and the federal Constitution. By the 1930s the British Privy Council likewise had developed into a judicial body that passed upon the validity of laws adopted in the British Commonwealth's dominions and in Britain's colonies. But the United States was the only major nation in which a judicial body, the Supreme Court, adjudicated the constitutionality of acts of a coordinate legislative body, Congress. Most notably, the Privy Council never addressed the validity of legislation adopted by what everyone understood to be its superior, the Westminster Parliament.

Prior to 1920, only a few other nations, nearly all in Latin America, had adopted judicial review. Argentina, Brazil, Colombia, Mexico, Venezuela, and even small nations like the Dominican Republic, among others, fell under the influence of US constitutional ideas in the mid-nineteenth century and incorporated variants of *Marbury v. Madison* into their constitutional systems. Alexis de Tocqueville's *Democracy in America*, which emphasized the central role of judges in American politics, played a fundamental role in this transfer of judicial review to other Western Hemisphere nations.

Movement in the direction of embracing judicial review began occurring in Europe in the aftermath of World War I, as the defeated Central Powers adopted and administered new constitutions. The first European nation to adopt any form of judicial review following the war was Czechoslovakia, although the Constitutional Tribunal created by its 1920 constitution never developed effective jurisdiction over claims of unconstitutionality and disappeared in 1938. Of greater significance was the tribunal established by the Austrian constitution of 1920, under the guidance of Austria's leading jurisprudential figure, Professor Hans Kelsen, who also served as a member of the Constitutional Tribunal until 1929. The 1920 Austrian constitution expressly established the principle of its own supremacy and conferred jurisdiction on the Constitutional Tribunal to declare invalid any inconsistent legislation.

Nonetheless, prior to the reinstitution of judicial review following the separation of Austria from Germany in 1945 and to constitutional reforms in 1975, the Austrian variant of judicial review was an insipid replica of the vibrant American practice. The key limitations in Austria resulted from narrow standing requirements, which authorized only specific judicial and other governmental institutions, within three years after the passage of any statute, to challenge its constitutionality. If proceedings were not commenced by appropriate officials within the appropriate time frame, the validity of a statute no longer could be challenged.

Something more analogous to *Marbury v. Madison* occurred in Weimar Germany. The 1919 Weimar Constitution created a Tribunal of State Justice, with jurisdiction over constitutional disputes between two or more *Lander*, or states, or between the national government and a *Land*. The tribunal was also empowered to try allegations that the president, the chancellor, or any minister had violated the constitution. In addition, the Tribunal of the Reich, the highest court in the ordinary judiciary, received jurisdiction to adjudicate the compatibility of legislation enacted by the *Lander* with imperial legislation. These provisions left a gap, however: no institution was charged with determining the compatibility of imperial legislation with the imperial constitution. In language akin to that of John Marshall in *Marbury*, the Tribunal of the Reich declared in a 1925 decision that "the submission of the judge to the law" implied "the power of the judge to question the validity of statutes of the Empire . . . when they are in opposition to other preeminent dispositions that must be observed by the judge," notably "the Imperial Constitution."

But this decision was heavily criticized, and thus the place of judicial review in German law remained unclear up to 1933, when Hitler came to power. It is noteworthy that no one sought to employ the doctrine to protect individual rights against Nazi atrocities. With Hitler's rise to power and Germany's subsequent subjugation of Austria and Czechoslovakia, review of legislation by an independent judiciary was squelched in Central Europe.

Thus, at the outset of World War II, the institution of judicial review existed mainly in the Western Hemisphere and functioned vibrantly only in the United States. Since 1945, however, constitutional practice has changed, and judicial review has spread worldwide. This chapter will examine the adoption of this most distinctive of American constitutional practices and explain its global acceptance.

Part of the explanation lies in the power and prestige of the United States. Throughout the nineteenth century, Europeans understandably regarded the United States as a cultural and intellectual backwater, and few European legal thinkers paid significant attention to America's legal and constitutional routines. But World War II transformed the position of the United States in the world. Its economic and military prowess commanded respect. Scholars from around the world began to study the legal, political, and constitutional practices of the United States, often at first hand and with financial support from American institutions. And, Americans began to advise foreigners who were drafting constitutions or otherwise to participate in the drafting process.

The former Axis powers were among the first to adopt judicial review. The Japanese Constitution of 1946, initially drafted by a committee of Americans in the office of General Douglas MacArthur, the commander of the American occupation army in Japan, explicitly gave the Supreme Court "power to determine the constitutionality of any law, order, regulation or official act," and the Court has exercised the power with the observation that it grew out of "interpretation of the American Constitution." Thus, there is little doubt that Japan copied the institution of judicial review from the United States, under the guidance of American thinkers and in the shadow of American military power.

Although Germans drafted the 1949 constitution of the Federal Republic of Germany—the constitution that remains in force in Germany today, American pressure and influence were not absent.

As the dominant victor in World War II and the emerging leader of the NATO coalition against the pretensions of the Soviet Union, the United States prodded the drafters of the 1949 constitution to commit Germany to the rule of law under the protection of an independent judiciary. The result was the creation of the Federal Constitutional Tribunal, which during the past half century has become, along with the Supreme Court of the United States, the most activist constitutional court in the world and has rendered some of the most important and interesting decisions of any such court.

Italy had been the third member of the Axis coalition. Although American military power had been highly instrumental in its defeat, Italy, unlike Germany and Japan, was not under military occupation in 1948 when it decided to abolish its monarchy and draft a constitution for a republic. Thus, it is more difficult to pinpoint American influence in the drafting of the 1948 constitution, although the influence was not entirely absent. The Constitution of 1948 explicitly recognized the doctrine of judicial review of the acts of the national legislature, and the establishment of a constitutional court in 1956 brought the practice of judicial review to fruition.

Meanwhile, halfway around the world, the practice of judicial review was also expanding. When India achieved independence from Great Britain in 1947, the framers of its constitution provided for judicial review of acts of the national legislature that violated fundamental individual rights or infringed upon state powers. Neither American prestige nor American military power can explain this development, however. India's elite had been thoroughly indoctrinated with British legal, constitutional, and political ideals, often through attendance at leading English universities, and had little experience with the United States. The American military, which had liberated Italy and conquered Germany and Japan, had no presence whatever in India. Thus, it does not seem that India was adopting judicial review for the purpose of copying the American model.

A better hypothesis is that India embraced judicial review because it served an important need. The subcontinent contains numerous ethnic and religious minorities, which subsequent history has shown had every reason to fear repression at the hands of a national majority dominating the national legislature. Thus, India presented a classic case that would become increasingly frequent as the twentieth century progressed, in which judicial review was needed to protect the integrity and civil liberties of minority races, religions, and other groups.

Canada is another nation with deep ethnic and religious divisions in which judicial review has become vibrant. Canada owes its existence to the British North America Act of 1867, through which the Parliament at Westminster created a federation between the Roman Catholic, French-speaking colony of Quebec and the Protestant, English-speaking colony of Ontario and several smaller provinces. The 1867 act did not, however, give Canada full independence from Great Britain; in particular, the Privy Council in London continued until 1949 to possess jurisdiction to hear appeals from the highest court in Canada.

During the eighty-two years of Privy Council jurisdiction, Canada gained increasing de facto independence, and the Privy Council's role changed imperceptibly from one of enforcing Westminster's imperial policies to one of interpreting the North America Act, which had become Canada's constitution. Thus, the Privy Council almost became a court reviewing the constitutionality of the acts of a coordinate legislative branch of government, but since it was a foreign court, sitting in the capital of the former imperial master, it never quite took on that role.

With the end of Privy Council appeals, the Supreme Court of Canada became the ultimate interpreter of the meaning of the North America Act and thus, in effect, the holder of a power of judicial review. It kept a low profile, however, until the Canadian government decided in 1980 to pursue a "patriation" policy of removing all vestiges of British imperial authority from Canadian life, including the vestige that only Parliament in Westminster could amend the Canadian constitution. The Canadian Supreme Court then issued an important ruling on the procedures that the government had to follow in pursuing its policy—a policy that eventuated in the 1982 adoption of a Canadian Charter of Rights and Freedoms.

The Supreme Court of Canada has made the charter a frequent basis for declaring both national and provincial legislation unconstitutional. But the charter gives the Court only a limited power of judicial review, since section 33 of the charter gives both the national and provincial legislatures power to override any court decision. This override has been used only once since 1982 outside Quebec and is, politically speaking, virtually unusable outside that province. But the Quebec assembly has used it with some frequency. Most importantly, when the Court struck down a Quebec law requiring French-only advertising signs as a violation of the charter's guarantee of freedom of expression, the Quebec assembly overrode the Court's decision. In cases protecting the rights of women, aborigines, and homosexuals, in contrast, the Canadian Supreme Court has pursued judicial activism with greater success. Together with the actions of the Quebec assembly, these decisions illustrate the essential nature of late twentieth-century constitutionalism and judicial review. Unlike the constitutionalism proclaimed in *Marbury v. Madison*, that of the late twentieth century concerns the empowerment of discrete and insular ethnic, religious, and cultural minorities. When those minorities possess voting power in legislatures, like the Quebec assembly, contemporary constitutions encourage them to use it to protect their interests. But when groups lack legislative power, bills of rights and the practice of judicial review of the constitutionality of legislation give them another institution, the judiciary, to provide them with protection.

Another use of a judicial body to deal with ethnic and cultural conflict has occurred in Belgium, which is divided roughly evenly between Flemish-speaking people in the North and French-speaking people in the South. As a result of reforms occurring in 1970 and 1980, Belgium created a court of arbitration, consisting of six Flemish-speaking and six French-speaking members, representing the two groups in the nation. In essence, the court has jurisdiction to declare unconstitutional legislation infringing the reserved rights of either of the groups.

The most recent constitution created for the purpose of protecting a minority is that of South Africa. When the apartheid regime agreed to yield power to a government elected by South Africa's black majority, it did so only on condition that the rights of the white minority be solidly entrenched in the new constitutional order. Many devices in South Africa's constitution entrench white rights and ensure that whites will continue to possess substantial power in the new regime. Here we need to be concerned only with the explicit conferral of power on South Africa's highest court to invalidate legislation that conflicts with rights, especially property rights, protected by the constitution. Through judicial maintenance of their property under the doctrine of judicial review, white South Africans have been made to feel assured that they will not become a powerless minority in their country, even if they are a discrete and insular one.

Thus, the doctrine of judicial review as proclaimed in *Marbury v. Madison* and altered by the US Supreme Court during the next century and a half began in the aftermath of World War II to spread around the globe. In part, especially in Germany and Japan, American military power and the prestige of the United States as a functioning democratic polity furthered the spread. But it also spread because the Supreme Court's transformation of the doctrine into a device for the protection of ethnic, religious, and cultural minorities gave it a purpose in the world of today that the original doctrine promulgated in *Marbury* had never enjoyed.

On other occasions during the second half of the twentieth century, judicial review spread for a variety of reasons connected to the specific political needs of the entities adopting it and to a general sense that the experience of the United States demonstrated the doctrine's utility in preserving democratic stability. But explicit pressure from the United States was absent. This was the case in 1950, when the Council of Europe adopted the European Convention for the Protection of Human Rights and Fundamental Freedoms, pursuant to which the European Court of Human Rights was established. It also was true seven years later when the Treaty of Rome created the European Economic Community, which later morphed into the European Union, and endowed it with a supreme judicial body, the European Court of Justice, with jurisdiction to determine whether acts of the EU's political bodies and acts of member states are consistent with the Union's fundamental charter.

Since the 1950s, many individual nations also have adopted judicial review for reasons connected to their own specific political needs, other than the protection of discrete and insular minorities. France is one of these nations. With the establishment of the Fifth Republic in 1958, France created a constitutional council, consisting of nine specially chosen judges plus any living former presidents of the Republic. The council is charged with a number of tasks including the determination of whether legislation is in "conformity with the Constitution . . . before its promulgation."

Other Western European states also have adopted judicial review in one form or another during the past half century. Thus, the Spanish constitution of 1978 reestablished the system of judicial review that had been briefly introduced in the short-lived republican constitution of 1931. The Portuguese constitution of 1976 also adopted judicial review, while Sweden adhered to the practice during the course of the 1970s.

Judicial review finally has penetrated even into the former Communist states of Eastern Europe. Yugoslavia created a constitutional court, which is now defunct, in 1962. Czechoslovakia established such a court in 1968, and both the Czech Republic and Slovakia continue to maintain constitutional courts today. But the main developments occurred as Communist power collapsed in the late 1980s and early 1990s: constitutional courts were established in Hungary in 1990, Romania in 1991, Lithuania in 1992, Belarus in 1994, and Latvia and Ukraine in 1996.

Most important of all was the constitutional court created in Russia in 1991. It initially assumed a strongly activist stance, passing on the constitutionality, inter alia, of President Boris Yeltsin's effort to suppress the Chechen rebellion of the mid-1990s and invalidating the legislation requiring Russia's citizens to carry passes while engaged in internal travel. It also appears to have survived Yeltsin's apparent attempt in 1993 to destroy it by forcing the resignation of its presiding judge and packing it with several new judges. But, while it technically remains in existence, it has lost independence during the rule of Vladimir Putin and often functions today under executive influence.

Perhaps the ultimate evidence of the global expansion of judicial review lies in the adoption of bills of rights even by nations that have remained committed to the doctrine of legislative supremacy. New Zealand offers an illustration. In 1985, New Zealand's deputy prime minister proposed adoption of a bill of rights, modeled on the Canadian Charter of Rights and Freedoms, with full-scale, *Marbury*-style judicial review. Opposition to judicial review, however, was strong, and New Zealand finally enacted its new bill of rights in 1990 as an ordinary statute, with an explicit provision that it did not render any other legislative enactment void or ineffective. The New Zealand Court of Appeal has obeyed this restriction, but some of its judges nonetheless have found it appropriate to declare some legislation incompatible with the bill of rights, even while leaving the legislation in force.

The effect of such declarations of incompatibility is remarkably close to the effect of Canadian declarations of unconstitutionality, which, it will be recalled, are subject to legislative override. In both instances, legislators come under political pressure to conform their statute to the requirements of justice—in Canada, by not overriding the judiciary's decision and in New Zealand, by repealing offending legislation. The difference, of course, is that in Canada the legislature must take action to override, while in New Zealand the legislature must take steps to repeal. Procedurally, this difference sometimes can affect results, but in the end the difference is not fundamental. Both the Canadian and the New Zealand approaches protect ultimate legislative supremacy, while at the same time making it difficult for the legislature to exercise that supremacy.

The ultimate source of the concept of legislative supremacy is, of course, English constitutional theory. And it is fitting that *Marbury v. Madison* and the doctrine of judicial review may be starting to triumph even in the halls of Westminster, with Parliament's passage of the Human Rights Act of 1998. Like New Zealand's bill of rights, Britain's Human Rights Act leaves incompatible legislation in force. But the act, like New Zealand's, does direct judges to strive to interpret other legislation to be consistent with the Human Rights Act, and it also opens the possibility that judges may find it appropriate to declare legislation incompatible, even while leaving it in force. A hope was that the Human Rights Act would lead to dialogue between Parliament and the judiciary, but so far little dialogue has occurred as Parliament has merely accepted judicial decisions and done what is minimally necessary to comply with them.

The Relevance of *Marbury* to Judicial Review Today

Should fidelity to the past—in particular, to the intentions of the Founding Fathers—compel judges in the twenty-first century to apply the doctrine of judicial review in the narrow, nonpolitical fashion adumbrated by Chief Justice Marshall in *Marbury v. Madison?* Should judges today distinguish between law and politics, limit themselves to deciding only questions of law, and avoid deciding questions of social policy? Or should we understand that judges in constitutional cases have broad power to strike down legislation on the basis of flexible standards of justice protective of discrete and insular minorities and on the basis of policies designed to bring those standards of justice to fruition?

Several arguments can be advanced in favor of remaining faithful to the original intentions of the Founding Fathers.

One argument is that Americans who lived in the late eighteenth and early nineteenth centuries possessed proper substantive values and established the Constitution and the federal government on the basis of those values. Americans of that era, it has been said, were Lockean individualists, or alternatively, were Republican communitarians who cared about their fellow citizens' rights and needs. Judges in the twenty-first century, according to this argument, should follow precedent and abide by the intentions of the founding generation because their doing so will ensure our continued governance in accordance with the Founders' sound substantive values.

A second argument focuses on the personal qualities rather than the substantive values of the founding generation. According to this argument, the men who drafted the Constitution, procured its ratification, and made the early decisions about how to put it into practice were more intelligent and disinterested than the people who ascend to positions of power and authority today. On balance, this greater intelligence and disinterestedness produced better decisions than those that would now be made by judges and political leaders acting on the basis of their own substantive views. It follows that the greater the guidance which today's leaders and judges accept from the past the better their decisions will be.

The third argument—and probably the central one—in favor of fidelity to the Founders does not assume that the past was better than or the founding generation was somehow superior to the present. Instead, its foundational principle is that it is illegitimate, in terms of the democratic norms of American political culture, for judges to be making fundamental choices between competing social policies. Two distinct intellectual traditions support this core claim.

The first is legal positivism. Positivists understand law as a set of commands addressed by lawmakers to judges, among others. Those judges have the capacity to understand and the obligation to obey the commands. In particular, positivism demands that the commands of the people assembled in constitutional framing and ratifying conventions must trump the commands of ordinary legislatures. Although positivism is under challenge today in many jurisprudential circles, it nonetheless remains difficult to imagine what it would be like to live in a world in which the precepts of positivism—that duly constituted representative bodies of the people have power to issue commands that judges and other officials are bound to obey—did not hold some sway. The precepts underlying positivism still retain great power over our lives and our legal imaginations.

The second tradition is the classical legal convention of judicial neutrality. A judge, it is said, must not favor one party appearing before her over another but rather must treat all litigants in the same way. Indeed, federal judges take an oath to "administer justice without respect to persons, and do equal right to the poor and to the rich." As individual litigants have come to represent the interests of larger groups or classes, it has become equally clear that judges should not show favoritism toward any particular group or class. Above all, it is urged that judges should never derive decisions from their own systems of value or their own preferences for one rather than another social policy.

Judges, the argument continues, are insufficiently attuned to democratic values to make policy choices on behalf of the people. Although politics does play a role in judicial selection processes, federal judges and judges in many states are not elected officials and thus have never had to reveal their policy preferences to the electorate and obtain the electorate's ratification of their policies. Even in states where judges are elected, they almost never reveal how they would decide specific policy questions. Moreover, judges typically hold office for lengthy terms—indeed, in the federal system and in some states, for life or until retirement. By the time judges are nearing the end of their term in office, it is thought, they have grown even more distant from popular, democratic processes of policy choice. The end result, it is feared, is that judges will make social policy choices without regard to the wishes of the electorate and to the democratic norm that the people themselves should determine the laws and policies by which they are governed.

Sophisticated thinkers who argue in favor of fidelity to the Founding Fathers do not doubt that judges on some occasions must make some policy choices and that the choices they make sometimes will preclude democratic political processes from making other choices. Sophisticated thinkers understand that, in creating precedent, judges inevitably make choices—that when judges engage in common law decision making in contract and tort cases, for example, they engage in interstitial policy making. But, those thinkers add, the legislature has the capacity by a simple majority vote to overturn the judiciary's policy choices in such cases, and its failure to vote to overturn can be understood as a sort of tacit, democratic acceptance of the choices the judges have made.

Similarly, thinkers who argue in favor of fidelity to the Founders understand that judicial obedience to the past in constitutional cases may preclude present, democratic majorities from making the policy choices they now desire. But it is essential, they emphasize, for judges to remain neutral and impartial by avoiding policy questions. They note, moreover, that it is not the policy choice of judges that prevents a present democratic majority from enacting the policies it desires; it is a past, democratic supermajority that is preventing the current democratic majority from enacting certain laws. And it is noted that, if a present democratic supermajority wanted to do so, it could change the Constitution, overturn what the past supermajority had decided, and abolish the constitutional limitations it had imposed.

John Marshall, as we have seen, incorporated many of these values into his *Marbury v. Madison* opinion. In light of his training in eighteenth-century legal and political theory, he fully appreciated the view of nearly all Americans that judges should not decide contested issues of social policy. The only proper role for judges, according to the logic of the *Marbury* opinion, was to follow established common law rules, to follow legislation when it altered the common law, and to follow the Constitution if it conflicted with legislation. Marshall understood that, if judges adhered to such a role, they would never decide policy issues but would only give effect to past decisions in which the people had acquiesced either through the legislative process or through their sovereign role as constitution makers.

Such an interpretation of *Marbury v. Madison* thus incorporates some very basic assumptions about American law and politics. On this interpretation of *Marbury*, it is impossible to make any sense of John Marshall's opinion or of judicial review except against a background assumption that the duty of judges, especially in constitutional cases, is to decide questions of law and abstain from politics. On this reading, judges are obliged to avoid policy issues, to defer to the legislature when such issues arise, and to invalidate legislation as unconstitutional only if they can ground their judgment in the text of the Constitution or in the clear intentions of the founding generation.

Marbury itself, as we have seen, arguably can be defended as a case in which the Supreme Court avoided policy issues, focused on the text of the Constitution, and thus rendered a legal as distinguished from a political decision. It is also possible to defend property rights cases as late as the end of the nineteenth century as involving mere protection of established legal rights codified by the Constitution's text in the Fifth and Fourteenth Amendments. Although the property rights cases, from the perspective of progressive reformers, involved policy choice, the justices who decided them could have viewed themselves as continuing in a narrow Marshallian tradition and applying nothing more than established law.

There are counterarguments, however, to this narrow style of judicial review emphasizing fidelity to the intentions of the Founders. The first counterargument arises out of the broad, highly political character that many judicial review cases had assumed as of 1787–

1788—the time of the framing and ratification of the Constitution. As of those years, judicial review had not yet taken on the narrow, apolitical style that Chief Justice Marshall gave it in *Marbury*. In the Stamp Act cases and writs of assistance cases of the late 1760s, the issues of constitutionality decided by the courts were at the heart of highly public, contentious conflicts between Great Britain and its American colonies over which the empire ultimately broke apart. Although some state cases in the 1780s aroused little public attention, publicly contentious cases such as *Rutgers v. Waddington* and *Trevett v. Weeden* continued to arise during that decade and to present fundamental issues of social policy. The historical record, which contains both narrow legalistic cases and broad, controversial political ones, is simply too ambiguous to establish what kind of judicial review, narrowly legal or broadly policy-oriented, the Constitution's framers had in mind when they adopted judicial review by giving the Supreme Court jurisdiction to review state-court judgments. Although the framers' generation distrusted policy making, the framers had to be aware that judges had made policy decisions in the Stamp Act cases and in some 1780s cases. As a result, it is impossible to conclude with confidence that the framers assumed that all judicial review cases would be purely legal in character, totally apolitical, and noncontroversial.

It follows that the narrow style of judicial review adopted by Marshall in *Marbury* is not mandated by a positivist claim that the framers and later the people in drafting and ratifying the Constitution commanded the judiciary to avoid making policy choices in future instances of judicial review. Those who framed and ratified the Constitution did not limit the sort of judicial review in which future judges could engage. Some different sort of originalism or special respect for the Founding Fathers—some belief in the moral or intellectual superiority of John Marshall and other Founders—is necessary to support a claim that respect for the past requires judges to adhere to *Marbury*'s narrow, nonpolitical style of judicial review.

Of course, the principle of judicial neutrality, together with an understanding that policy choice can never be a neutral process, supports adherence to narrow, nonpolitical judicial review.

But that only brings us to a second counterargument. This second argument rests on an observation that most cases of judicial review today differ profoundly from the sorts of cases decided in the era of *Marbury*. Judicial review at the time of *Marbury* was designed to protect common law rights, especially rights of property—rights that had been established during the course of hundreds of years of adjudication and were widely accepted in the early 1800s. Fixed rules of law supported by a broad consensus existed in regard to those rights, and courts could readily turn to those rules to maintain the rights and thereby avoid political questions about the desirability and degree of social change.

Today, in contrast, many cases of judicial review involve issues of minority rights. What sorts of minorities are sufficiently discrete and insular to merit strict judicial scrutiny? Women? Gay people? Transgender people? Poor people? The people of Appalachia? Or only people of color? How much special solicitude should these different minorities receive? Should some receive greater solicitude than others? Most of these questions are new ones for which little law or precedent exists. Moreover, the constitutional text on which decisions must be based—section one of the Fourteenth Amendment—is a paragon of ambiguity. It is thus difficult to see how judges can decide most questions of minority rights without recourse to political decision making about issues of social policy.

Perhaps the ultimate policy issue facing government today is whether discrete and insular minorities should receive special protection at all and be assimilated into the political and social mainstream. Or should a society's dominant groups be left free to govern their polity in their own interest and to discriminate against minorities to whatever extent they deem appropriate? Was Senator Robert Wagner correct that the most important task of just government today is the protection of minority rights? If Wagner was correct, it inevitably follows that legislatures under the control of majorities are not the best institution for protecting minority rights, that courts will need to provide much of that protection, and that judges will need to confront the policy questions involved in determining the right amount of protection.

The answer to this ultimate policy issue is not the same for all societies at all times. Nor do judges need to resolve it; the issue, in large part, is resolved for them in most places at most times. The narrow form of judicial review practiced in early nineteenth-century America was irrelevant to the rest of the world in the nineteenth century, and thus most of the rest of the world ignored it. Other nations did not need a judiciary to serve as a bulwark of property rights against redistributive onslaughts from the political left—the most significant function that the doctrine performed in the United States. In most of nineteenth-century Europe, in contrast, a monarch, a hereditary nobility, and an established church, all with extensive landholdings, were able to protect their own property rights as well as the entrepreneurial rights of the growing bourgeoisie. Europeans in the nineteenth century did not need *Marbury* and hence did not adopt judicial review. Similarly, there are few nations in the world that need judicial review today in order to protect property rights.

Judicial review is important today because it gives effect to a principle of justice that began to emerge in Western democracies in the late 1930s and since then has been accepted by many Americans and people of other nations—a principle that racial, religious, and comparable forms of discrimination are profoundly evil and unjust. Hitler, the Holocaust, and genocide have become humanity's paradigms of iniquity. And judicial review has become the institutional mechanism through which societies can advance policies that promote justice, equality, and assimilation and prevent injustice and discrimination.

Judicial review for the protection of minority rights is in place, by constitutional text or established constitutional practice, in much of the world today. Judges engage in it and, in doing so, make the policy choices involved in determining the nature and extent of protection. Such policy choice is inevitable once one assumes that racial, religious, and comparable forms of discrimination are evil and unjust; that legislatures chosen through majoritarian, democratic processes lack the impartiality to provide the protection that victims of discrimination deserve; and that only judges are sufficiently insulated from majority prejudices to be trusted to provide protection.

But judicial policy making has its costs. Every policy decision judges make calls their impartiality into question and leads the electorate to demand the selection of judges who agree with majority views. Judges who are so selected become only marginally better than legislators in protecting minorities. Although judges do not need to seek reelection or reappointment as frequently as legislators do, if they need to seek it at all, and thus can be more independent of political majorities than legislators can be, many judges retain ties to those who supported their elevation to the bench and sacrifice impartiality as a result.

John Marshall thus displayed profound wisdom when he recognized that the power of judges depends on their impartial adjudication of issues of law and their avoidance of political issues of social policy. However, because protection of minorities involves inevitable policy choices, judges today cannot totally avoid policy making. The protection of minority rights and judicial impartiality are simply in tension with each other, and judges must make an ultimate policy judgment about how much weight to give to each.

1700–1760   Courts and juries periodically nullify legislative acts.

1755   Birth of John Marshall.

1761   James Otis argues *Writs of Assistance Case*.

1764   James Otis publishes *The Rights of the British Colonies Asserted and Proved*.

1765–1766   American judges declare Stamp Act unconstitutional.

1775–1783   War for Independence.

1780s   State judges consider their power to hold legislative acts unconstitutional.

1787   Constitutional Convention implicitly upholds power of judicial review.

1790s   Federal and state judges periodically hold legislative acts, including those of Congress, unconstitutional.

1800   Thomas Jefferson defeats John Adams in presidential election.

1801   Adams appoints John Marshall as chief justice of the US Supreme Court.

1801   Federalist Congress adopts Judiciary Act and John Adams appoints Federalist judges.

1802   Jeffersonian Congress repeals 1801 Judiciary Act.

1803   *Marbury v. Madison* and *Stuart v. Laird* decided.

1810   *Fletcher v. Peck* decided.

1819   *Dartmouth College Case* decided.

1825   *Eakin v. Raub* decided.

1856   *Wynehamer v. People* decided.

1857   *Scott v. Sandford* decided.

1905   *Lochner v. New York* decided.

1938   *United States v. Carolene Products Co.* decided.

1946   Japanese Constitution adopts judicial review.

1947   Indian Constitution adopts judicial review.

1949	German Basic Law adopts judicial review.
1982	Canadian Charter of Rights and Freedoms adopted.
1998	Human Rights Act directs British courts to interpret all legislation consistently with human rights.

BIBLIOGRAPHICAL ESSAY

Note from the Series Editors: The following bibliographical essay contains the major primary and secondary sources the author consulted for this volume. We have asked all authors in the series to omit formal citations in order to make our volumes more readable, inexpensive, and appealing for students and general readers. In adopting this format, Landmark Law Cases and American Society follows the precedent of a number of highly regarded and widely consulted series.

Marbury v. Madison is reported at 1 Cranch (5 U.S.) 137 (1803). For classic interpretations of the case by progressive historians, see Albert J. Beveridge, *The Life of John Marshall*, 4 vols. (Boston: Houghton Mifflin, 1916–1919); Felix Frankfurter, *The Commerce Clause under Marshall, Taney and Waite* (Chapel Hill: University of North Carolina Press, 1937); and Charles Warren, *The Supreme Court in United States History*, 2 vols. (Boston: Little Brown, 1922). For more recent interpretations in the same mold, see Robert G. Mc-Closkey, *The American Supreme Court* (Chicago: University of Chicago Press, 1960); J. M. Sosin, *The Aristocracy of the Long Robe: The Origins of Judicial Review in America* (Westport, CT: Greenwood Press, 1989); and Christopher L. Eisgruber, "John Marshall's Judicial Rhetoric," *1996 Supreme Court Review* (Chicago: University of Chicago Press, 1997), 439. In a more recent article, Christopher L. Eisgruber, "*Marbury*, Marshall, and the Politics of Constitutional Judgment," *Virginia Law Review* 89 (2003): 1203, which challenges the interpretation of *Marbury* put forward in this book, Eisgruber proposes a subtle distinction between political will, as exercised by legislative and executive figures, and judicial judgment, which contains political but not partisan elements. Eisgruber may, in fact, be offering an apt description of what ideally differentiates judicial judgment from politics today. In my view, however, Marshall was writing for an audience that was not interested in the sorts of subtlety of concern to today's jurisprudes, but needed to be persuaded simply that the Supreme Court would not engage in political decision making such as that in which Stamp Act courts and some 1780s courts had engaged.

Most recent scholarship tends to place the *Marbury* decision in the context of late eighteenth- and early nineteenth-century politics and ideas. Three classic works on mid- to late eighteenth-century political theory are Bernard Bailyn, *The Ideological Origins of the American Revolution* (Cambridge, MA: Harvard University Press, 1967); John Phillip Reid, *Constitutional History of the American Revolution* (Madison: University of Wisconsin Press, 1995); and Gordon S. Wood, *The Creation of the American Republic, 1776–1787* (Chapel Hill: University of North Carolina Press, 1969). The scholarship during recent decades that places *Marbury* in the theoretical context elucidated by these books includes Robert Lowry Clinton, *Marbury v. Madison and Judicial Review* (Lawrence: University Press of Kansas, 1989); Charles F. Hobson, *The Great Chief Justice: John Marshall and the Rule of Law* (Lawrence: University Press of Kansas, 1996); Larry D. Kramer, *The People Themselves: Popular Constitutionalism and Judicial Review* (New York: Oxford University Press, 2004); Sylvia Snowiss, *Judicial Review and the Law of the Constitution* (New Haven, CT: Yale University Press, 1990); James M. O'Fallon, "Marbury," *Stanford Law Review* 44 (1992): 219; William E. Nelson, "The Eighteenth-Century Background of John Marshall's Constitutional Jurisprudence," *Michigan Law Review* 76 (1978): 893; and William Michael Treanor, "Judicial Review before Marbury," *Stanford Law Review* 58 (2005): 455. Four other noteworthy articles are Mary Sarah Bilder, "The Corporate Origins of Judicial Review," *Yale Law Journal* 116 (2006): 502; Michael Stokes Paulsen, "The Irrepressible Myth of Marbury," *Michigan Law Review* 101 (2003): 2706; G. Edward White, "The Constitutional Journey of Marbury v. Madison," *Virginia Law Review* 89 (2003): 1463; Louise Weinberg, "Our Marbury," *Virginia Law Review* 89 (2003): 1235.

A vast literature exists in regard to the social structure of the localities of eighteenth-century British North America. The best work includes T. H. Breen, *Tobacco Culture: The Mentality of the Great Planters on the Eve of Revolution* (Princeton, NJ: Princeton University Press, 1985); Edward M. Cook Jr., *The Fathers of the Towns: Leadership and Community Structure in Eighteenth-Century New England* (Baltimore: Johns Hopkins University Press, 1976); Edward Countryman, *A People in Revolution: The American Revolution and Political Society in New York, 1760–1790* (Baltimore: Johns Hopkins University Press, 1981); Rhys Isaac, *The Transformation of Virginia, 1740–1790* (Chapel Hill: University of North Carolina Press, 1982); Rachel N. Klein, *Unification of a Slave State: The Rise of the Planter Class in the South Carolina Backcountry, 1760–1808* (Chapel Hill: University of North Carolina Press, 1990); Gary B. Nash, *The Urban Crucible: Social Change, Political Consciousness, and the Origins of the American Revolution* (Cambridge, MA: Harvard University Press, 1979); William M. Offutt, *Law and Society in the Delaware Valley, 1680–1710* (Champaign: University of Illinois Press, 1995); Darrett B. Rutman and Anita H. Rutman, *A Place in Time: Middlesex County, Virginia, 1650–1750* (New York: W.W. Norton, 1984); and Michael Zuckerman, *Peaceable Kingdoms: New England Towns in the Eighteenth Century* (New York: Alfred A. Knopf, 1970).

On the role of eighteenth-century courts and juries in the context of this social structure, I have relied mainly on my own earlier work, William E. Nelson, *Americanization of the Common Law: The Impact of Legal Change on Massachusetts Society, 1760–1830* (Cambridge, MA: Harvard University Press, 1975) and William E. Nelson, *The Common Law in Colonial America*, 4 vols. (New York: Oxford University Press, 2008–2017), but also on

F. Thornton Miller, *Juries and Judges versus the Law: Virginia's Provincial Legal Perspective, 1783–1828* (Charlottesville: University Press of Virginia, 1994); Gwenda Morgan, *The Hegemony of the Law: Richmond County, Virginia, 1692–1776* (New York: Garland Publishing, 1989); and Deborah A. Rosen, *Courts and Commerce: Gender, Law and the Market Economy in Colonial New York* (Columbus: Ohio State University Press, 1997). For reasons stated in the preface to the 1994 edition of William E. Nelson, *Americanization of the Common Law: The Impact of Legal Change on Massachusetts Society, 1760–1830* (Athens: University of Georgia Press, 1994), at xii–xiii, I continue to reject the position of Bruce H. Mann, *Neighbors and Strangers: Law and Community in Early Connecticut* (Chapel Hill: University of North Carolina Press, 1987), that the power of juries to find law as well as fact declined in the early and mid-eighteenth century.

Three books that together provide the best overview of government and politics for the entire 1760–1815 period are Robert Middlekauff, *The Glorious Cause: The American Revolution, 1763–1789* (New York: Oxford University Press, 1982); Stanley Elkins and Eric McKitrick, *The Age of Federalism: The Early American Republic, 1788–1800* (New York: Oxford University Press, 1993); and Gordon S. Wood, *Empire of Liberty: A History of the Early Republic, 1789–1815* (New York: Oxford University Press, 2009). For the period leading up to the War for Independence, Bernard Bailyn, *The Ideological Origins of the American Revolution* (Cambridge, MA: Harvard University Press, 1967), and Merrill Jensen, *The Founding of a Nation: A History of the American Revolution* (New York: Oxford University Press, 1968), remain vital and offer competing interpretations. On the war years themselves, Piers Mackesy, *The War for America, 1775–1783* (Cambridge, MA: Harvard University Press, 1964), and Charles Royster, *A Revolutionary People at War: The Continental Army and American Character, 1775–1783* (Chapel Hill: University of North Carolina Press, 1979), are recommended. For the Confederation period, see Merrill Jensen, *The Articles of Confederation* (Madison: University of Wisconsin Press, 1940), and Jack N. Rakove, *The Beginnings of National Politics: An Interpretive History of the Continental Congress* (New York: Alfred A. Knopf, 1979), again for differing interpretations. On the process leading up to the adoption of the federal Constitution, three classics are Max Farrand, *The Framing of the Constitution of the United States* (New Haven, CT: Yale University Press, 1913); Forrest McDonald, *We the People: The Economic Origins of the Constitution* (Chicago: University of Chicago Press, 1958), and Gordon Wood, *The Creation of the American Republic, 1776–1787* (Chapel Hill: University of North Carolina Press, 1969).

On the role of lawyers in colonial government and politics, I have relied mainly on my recent work, William E. Nelson, *The Common Law in Colonial America*, 4 vols. (New York: Oxford University Press, 2008–2017). For the transformation of lawyers into leaders of opposition to the Crown, I have relied especially on William E. Nelson, *The Common Law in Colonial America*, vol. 4: *American Law on the Eve of Independence, 1735–1776* (New York: Oxford University Press, 2017). Older work includes Edmund S. Morgan and Helen M. Morgan, *The Stamp Act Crisis: Prologue to Revolution*, rev. ed. (New York: Collier Books, 1963); M. H. Smith, *The Writs of Assistance Case* (Berkeley: University of California Press, 1978); Bernard Bailyn, "Introduction to James Otis, 'The Rights of the British Colonies Asserted and Proved,'" in *Pamphlets of the American Revolution*, ed. Bernard Bailyn (Cambridge, MA: Harvard University Press, 1965), 408.

On early judicial review in the states, the most comprehensive recent source is William Michael Treanor, "Judicial Review before Marbury," *Stanford Law Review* 58 (2005): 455. See also Peter C. Hoffer, *Rutgers v. Waddington: Alexander Hamilton, the End of the War for Independence, and the Origins of Judicial Review* (Lawrence: University Press of Kansas, 2016); Daniel J. Hulsebosch, "A Discrete and Cosmopolitan Minority: The Loyalists, the Atlantic World, and the Origins of Judicial Review," *Chicago-Kent Law Review* 81 (2006): 825; William E. Nelson, "Changing Conceptions of Judicial Review: The Evolution of Constitutional Theory in the States," *University of Pennsylvania Law Review* 120 (1972): 1166–1185; James Bradley Thayer, "The Origin and Scope of the American Doctrine of Constitutional Law," *Harvard Law Review* 7 (1893): 129–156.

For some of the vast literature on government and politics in the 1790s, see Jerald A. Combs, *The Jay Treaty: Political Battleground of the Founding Fathers* (Berkeley: University of California Press, 1970); Noble E. Cunningham, *The Jeffersonian Republicans: The Formation of Party Organization, 1789–1801* (Chapel Hill: University of North Carolina Press, 1957); Manning J. Dauer, *The Adams Federalists* (Baltimore: Johns Hopkins University Press, 1953); E. James Ferguson, *The Power of the Purse: A History of American Public Finance, 1776–1790* (Chapel Hill: University of North Carolina Press, 1961); David C. Hendrickson, *Empire of Liberty: The Statecraft of Thomas Jefferson* (New York: Oxford University Press, 1990); Richard Hofstadter, *The Idea of a Party System: The Rise of Legitimate Opposition in the United States, 1780–1840* (Berkeley: University of California Press, 1969); Stephen G. Kurtz, *The Presidency of John Adams: The Collapse of Federalism, 1795–1800* (Philadelphia: University of Pennsylvania Press, 1957); Forrest McDonald, *Alexander Hamilton: A Biography* (New York: W. W. Norton, 1979); Clinton Rossiter, *Alexander Hamilton and the Constitution* (New York: Harcourt, Brace & World, 1964); and Leonard D. White, *The Federalists: A Study in Administrative History* (New York: Macmillan, 1948).

A different body of scholarship addresses the life of John Marshall, the author of *Marbury v. Madison*. The classic biography of Marshall is Albert J. Beveridge, *The Life of John Marshall*, 4 vols. (Boston: Houghton Mifflin, 1916–1919). The three most recent biographical treatments are Charles F.

Hobson, *The Great Chief Justice: John Marshall and the Rule of Law* (Lawrence: University Press of Kansas, 1996); Herbert A. Johnson, *The Chief Justiceship of John Marshall* (Columbia: University of South Carolina Press, 1997); and Jean Edward Smith, *John Marshall: Definer of a Nation* (New York: Henry Holt, 1996). Hobson's treatment is especially valuable, since Hobson is the editor of the John Marshall papers and he has included and discussed in his biography references to sources unused by previous biographers and historians. Two other useful biographies are Leonard Baker, *John Marshall: A Life in Law* (New York: Macmillan, 1974), and Francis N. Stites, *John Marshall: Defender of the Constitution* (Boston: Little, Brown, 1981).

The companion case to *Marbury*, which is *Stuart v. Laird*, is reported at 5 U.S. (1 Cranch) 299 (1803). The *Marbury* case and to a lesser extent the *Stuart* case have been the subjects of an enormous scholarly commentary. I have relied most heavily on my own article, William E. Nelson, "The Eighteenth-Century Background of John Marshall's Constitutional Jurisprudence," *Michigan Law Review* 76 (1978): 893–960, as well as on Robert Lowry Clinton, Marbury v. Madison *and Judicial Review* (Lawrence: University Press of Kansas, 1989); Donald O. Dewey, *Marshall versus Jefferson: The Political Background of* Marbury v. Madison (New York: Alfred A. Knopf, 1970); George L. Haskins and Herbert A. Johnson, *Foundations of Power: John Marshall, 1801–15* (New York: Macmillan, 1981); Charles F. Hobson, *The Great Chief Justice: John Marshall and the Rule of Law* (Lawrence: University Press of Kansas, 1996); Larry D. Kramer, *The People Themselves: Popular Constitutionalism and Judicial Review* (New York: Oxford University Press, 2004); Jean Edward Smith, *John Marshall: Definer of a Nation* (New York: Henry Holt, 1996); Sylvia Snowiss, *Judicial Review and the Law of the Constitution* (New Haven, CT: Yale University Press, 1990); J. M. Sosin, *The Aristocracy of the Long Robe: The Origins of Judicial Review in America* (Westport, CT: Greenwood Press, 1989); and William Van Alstyne, "A Critical Guide to *Marbury v. Madison*," *Duke Law Journal* 15 (1969): 1.

On the conflict between Federalists and Anti-Federalists, and later Federalists and Republicans, over the scope and power of the federal judiciary—the conflict at the root of *Marbury* and *Stuart*—see Saul Cornell, *The Other Founders: Anti-Federalism and the Dissenting Tradition in America, 1788–1828* (Chapel Hill: University of North Carolina Press, 1999); and Richard E. Ellis, *The Jeffersonian Crisis: Courts and Politics in the Young Republic* (New York: Oxford University Press, 1971).

The best discussion of the immediate reception of the *Marbury* case is contained in Jean Edward Smith, *John Marshall: Definer of a Nation* (New York: Henry Holt, 1996). For the impact of *Marbury* during the course of the nineteenth century's first two decades, I have relied most heavily on my own article, William E. Nelson, "The Eighteenth-Century Background of John Marshall's Constitutional Jurisprudence," *Michigan Law Review* 76 (1978):

893–960, as well as on Robert Lowry Clinton, *Marbury v. Madison and Judicial Review* (Lawrence: University Press of Kansas, 1989); George L. Haskins and Herbert A. Johnson, *Foundations of Power: John Marshall, 1801–15* (New York: Macmillan, 1981); Charles F. Hobson, *The Great Chief Justice: John Marshall and the Rule of Law* (Lawrence: University Press of Kansas, 1996); and J. M. Sosin, *The Aristocracy of the Long Robe: The Origins of Judicial Review in America* (Westport, CT: Greenwood Press, 1989). For analysis of judicial review in state courts in the late eighteenth and early nineteenth centuries, see William E. Nelson, "Changing Conceptions of Judicial Review: The Evolution of Constitutional Theory in the States, 1790–1860," *University of Pennsylvania Law Review* 120 (1972): 1166–1185, and the classic essay of James B. Thayer, "The Origin and Scope of the American Doctrine of Constitutional Law," *Harvard Law Review* 7 (1893): 129–156.

For analysis of the longer history of judicial review over the course of the nineteenth century, I have relied mainly on my own earlier work: William E. Nelson, *The Roots of American Bureaucracy, 1830–1900* (Cambridge, MA: Harvard University Press, 1982); William E. Nelson, "The Eighteenth-Century Background of John Marshall's Constitutional Jurisprudence," *Michigan Law Review* 76 (1978): 893–960; and William E. Nelson, "Changing Conceptions of Judicial Review: The Evolution of Constitutional Theory in the States, 1790–1860," *University of Pennsylvania Law Review* 120 (1972): 1166–1185. I continue to find Arnold M. Paul, *Conservative Crisis and the Rule of Law: Attitudes of Bench and Bar, 1887–1895* (Ithaca, NY: Cornell University Press, 1960), valuable. Other useful work includes James W. Ely Jr., *The Guardian of Every Other Right: A Constitutional History of Property Rights* (New York: Oxford University Press, 1992); Benjamin F. Wright, *The Growth of American Constitutional Law* (New York: Reynal & Hitchcock, 1942); Edward S. Corwin, "The Doctrine of Due Process before the Civil War," *Harvard Law Review* 24 (1911): 366–385, 460–479; Edward S. Corwin, "The Basic Doctrine of American Constitutional Law," *Michigan Law Review* 12 (1914): 247–276; and Charles G. Haines, "Judicial Review of Legislation in the United States and the Doctrine of Vested Rights and of Implied Limitations on Legislatures," *Texas Law Review* 2 (1924): 257–290, 387–421, and 3 (1924): 1–43.

Historians have long debated whether a sudden change occurred in the jurisprudence of the US Supreme Court in the late 1930s, what the nature of that change was, and why the change occurred. For recent variants of the conventional wisdom, which sees a conservative Supreme Court buckling under pressure from a liberal president and suddenly transforming its jurisprudence in the spring of 1937, see William E. Leuchtenburg, *The Supreme Court Reborn* (New York: Oxford University Press, 1995); Michael Ariens, "A Thrice-Told Tale, or Felix the Cat," *Harvard Law Review* 107 (1994): 620; Richard D. Friedman, "A Reaffirmation: The Authenticity of the Roberts Memorandum, or Felix the Non-Forger," *University of Pennsylvania Law*

Review 142 (1994): 1985; and Richard D. Friedman, "Switching Time and Other Thought Experiments: The Hughes Court and Constitutional Transformation," *University of Pennsylvania Law Review* 142 (1994): 1891. Bruce A. Ackerman, *We the People: Transformations* (Cambridge, MA: Harvard University Press, 1998), builds a complex argument that the 1937 change was so momentous that it enjoys the stature of a constitutional amendment. In contrast, Barry Cushman, *Rethinking the New Deal Court: The Structure of a Constitutional Revolution* (New York: Oxford University Press, 1998), argues that the change in the Court's jurisprudence was a gradual one, beginning in the 1920s and ending in the 1940s, that was more in the nature of common law accretion than constitutional transformation. For literature situating the jurisprudential changes of 1937–1938 in the context of Nazism in Europe and of American reactions to Nazism, see William E. Nelson, *The Legalist Reformation: Law, Politics, and Ideology in New York, 1920–1980* (Chapel Hill: University of North Carolina Press, 2001); Richard A. Primus, *The American Language of Rights* (New York: Cambridge University Press, 1999); Robert M. Cover, "The Origins of Judicial Activism in the Protection of Minorities," *Yale Law Journal* 91 (1982): 1287.

Many books have examined the global spread of judicial review. The old standard is Mauro Cappelletti, *Judicial Review in the Contemporary World* (Indianapolis: Bobbs-Merrill, 1971), but so many developments have occurred since its publication that it is now badly out-of-date. The most thorough recent book, which, however, also is becoming dated, is Allan R. Brewer-Carias, *Judicial Review in Comparative Law* (Cambridge: Cambridge University Press, 1989). Other books and articles of value include Rob Bakker, Aalt Willem Heringa, and Frits Stroink, eds., *Judicial Control: Comparative Essays on Judicial Review* (Apeldoorn, Netherlands: Maklu, 1995); David M. Beatty, ed., *Human Rights and Judicial Review: A Comparative Perspective* (Dordrecht: Martinus Nijhoff, 1994); Donald W. Jackson and C. Neal Tate, eds., *Comparative Judicial Review and Public Policy* (Westport, Ct.: Greenwood Press, 1992); Edward McWhinney, *Supreme Courts and Judicial Law-Making: Constitutional Tribunals and Constitutional Review* (Dordrecht: Martinus Nijhoff, 1986); C. Neal Tate and Torbjorn Vallinder, *The Global Expansion of Judicial Power* (New York: New York University Press, 1995); Carla Thorson, *Politics, Judicial Review and the Russian Constitutional Court* (New York: Palgrave Macmillan, 2012); Matthew Harris, "Is New Zealand Law Ready for a *Marbury v. Madison* Moment?," *New Zealand Universities Law Review* 25 (2012): 210; C. R. G. Murray, "The Continuation of Politics by Other Means: Judicial Dialogue under the Human Rights Act of 1998," in *The United Kingdom's Statutory Bill of Rights: Constitutional and Comparative Perspectives*, ed. Roger Masterman and Ian Leigh (Oxford: Oxford University Press, 2013), 51. Tom Alvarez, ed., *The Statesman's Year-Book: The Politics, Cultures and Economies of the World, 2017* (London: Palgrave Macmillan, 2016), contains a useful, although occasionally incomplete, nation-by-nation account of the constitutional courts that currently exist throughout the world.

Marbury v. Madison has enormous continuing significance to contemporary American constitutional law and constitutional theory. It is almost impossible to open a volume of a contemporary law review without finding at least one article addressed, at least tangentially, to the issue of how judges should decide constitutional cases. My own thinking on this issue was developed in William E. Nelson, "History and Neutrality in Constitutional Adjudication," *Virginia Law Review* 72 (1986): 1237, and my views in the conclusion are derived from that article.

Several works that also provide additional bibliographic guidance are Antonin Scalia, Amy Gutmann, Gordon S. Wood, Laurence H. Tribe, Mary Ann Glendon, and Ronald Dworkin, *A Matter of Interpretation: Federal Courts and the Law* (Princeton, NJ: Princeton University Press, 1997); Christopher L. Eisgruber, "Early Interpretations & Original Sins," *Michigan Law Review* 95 (1997): 2005; Barry Friedman and Scott B. Smith, "The Sedimentary Constitution," *University of Pennsylvania Law Review* 147 (1998): 1; Michael W. McConnell, "The Importance of Humility in Judicial Review: A Comment on Ronald Dworkin's 'Moral Reading' of the Constitution," *Fordham Law Review* 65 (1997): 1269. Most noteworthy among the classic works are John Hart Ely, *Democracy and Distrust: A Theory of Judicial Review* (Cambridge, MA: Harvard University Press, 1980); Robert H. Bork, "Neutral Principles and Some First Amendment Problems," *Indiana Law Journal* 47 (1971): 1; Paul Brest, "The Misconceived Quest for the Original Understanding," *Boston University Law Review* 60 (1980): 204; Michael J. Perry, "Interpretivism, Freedom of Expression, and Equal Protection," *Ohio State Law Journal* 42 (1981): 261; H. Jefferson Powell, "The Original Understanding of Original Intent," *Harvard Law Review* 98 (1985): 885; Mark V. Tushnet, "Following the Rules Laid Down: A Critique of Interpretivism and Neutral Principles," *Harvard Law Review* 96 (1983): 781; Herbert Wechsler, "Toward Neutral Principles of Constitutional Law," *Harvard Law Review* 73 (1959): 1.

INDEX

Hitler, Adolf, 131, 140, 153
Hobson, Charles, 4–5
Holmes v. Walton, 56, 61
Holocaust, 153
Human Rights Act of 1998, 146
Hungary, 145
Hutchinson, Thomas, 25
Hylton v. United States, 66–67

income tax, 124
Independent Reflector, 20, 35, 40
India, 141–142
Indians, 68–69
instructions, to jury, 12–13
interest groups, 131–133
international commerce, 71
Italy, 141

Jackson, Age of, 110
Jackson, Andrew, 2
Japan, 149
Jay, John, 75, 81, 86
Jay's Treaty, 75, 81, 83
Jefferson, Thomas, 13, 79
    as president, 87–88, 94, 96, 107
    as presidential candidate, 75, 77,
        85–86
Jehovah's Witnesses, 135
Jews, 21
Jordan v. Law, 48, 50
judges, 26–27
Judiciary Act of 1789, 92–93, 104
    section 13 of, 97, 99, 104, 114
Judiciary Act of 1801, 90, 93, 103,
    108
Judiciary Act of 1802, 93–94,
    103–104
juries, 83, 91–92
    power of, to determine law,
        11–17, 22, 28–29, 92

Kamper v. Hawkins, 111
Keith, Mary Randolph, 78

Kelsen, Hans, 139
Kent, James, 116
Kentucky and Virginia Resolutions,
    109
Key, V. O., 133
Keynes, John Maynard, 131
Knox, Raymond C., 131
Kramer, Larry D., 6, 43

Latvia, 145
law
    distinguished from politics, 8–9,
        24, 94–99, 102–105, 108,
        129–130, 136
    as fixed, 33–34, 74, 103, 111
legal realists, 2
legal tender, 59, 64
Lehman, Irving, 134
Lexington, Battle of, 69
Lithuania, 145
Livingston, William, 20
localism, 7, 11–22, 33
Long, Huey, 131
Lowdnes, Rawlins, 49
Lowi, Theodore, 133
Loyalists, 56–61, 64

MacArthur, Douglas, 140
Madison, James, 62–63, 73, 76, 93,
    98, 104
mandamus, 97–99
Marbury, William, 93, 97
Marcantonio, Vito, 131
Marshall, Thomas, 78
Martin, Luther, 101
Mason, George, 55, 63
Mason, William, 50
Massachusetts, 46–47
Matter of Jacobs, 125
McCloskey, Robert G., 2
McCullough v. Brown, 125
Mercer, John, 62
Mexico, 138